Totterdown Rising

KATE POLLARD

October 30, 1941 *to* January 2, 2009

To the Totterdown people who had to leave; to TAG's

direct action; to those who kept community life going;

and lastly to every other community which has been

disrupted by Mega-Planning Disasters

Angers Road in 1970. Courtesy Bristol Central Library

Published by Totterdown Press
Totterdown Press is an imprint of Tangent Books

5.16 Paintworks
Bristol BS4 3EH
0117 972 0645

www.tangentbooks.co.uk

Contents

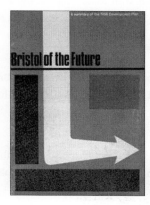

'Bristol of the Future' – cover of the 1966 Development
Plan Summary (Nigel Hall's archive)

Acknowledgements

I want to express deep gratitude to all of the following people and organisations who gave their time, support and material for the book. We have included all the photos – and many *Bristol Evening Post* photos – that we could in order to make this the best possible record of the events and of places in the Totterdown no longer with us. Particular thanks, then, to Gerry Brooke and the *Bristol Evening Post*. Without Gerry's involvement in direct action and setting up the Totterdown Action Group (TAG), events might have run a different course; also we would not have such a brilliant photographic record of those times. Sincere thanks to and for:

Photos
Bristol Evening Post's archive
Mike Leigh of Bristol Record Office for photos of Totterdown's redevelopment
Bristol University Theatre Collection images by Derek Balmer
Bristol Record Office, John Williams
Bristol Central Library (Local History) for permission to include their former Angers Road photo in the Dedication (thank goodness someone rushed out to take a photo before it was demolished)
Denys Chamberlain for Knowle Picture House archival photos
Paul and John Attwell for their Bushey Lodge photos
Nigel Hall for his personal Action Area work archive
Pat and Peter Wright for photos from their Three Lamps renovation archive
Shire Public Hall CA for long loan of their camera and of Shire Baptist Church's dictation software mediated by Ash Bearman when I got RSI!

To Reminiscers
Margaret and Jim Dudbridge, Ruth Brown, Anne Townsend and Kathleen Warren, Graham Davey, Vivien Pipping, Brenda Spriggs and Dulcie, Mr and Mrs McCloud, Clive Clifford, David Cox, Graham Spencer, Nigel Hall, Marilyn Webb, Sandra Mills, Anne Harding, Dave Winters, Mike Leigh, Sue Learner, John Grimshaw, Jean and Reg Piper, Denys Chamberlain.

For contributions and support from
Tony Benn for enigmatic comments; Mike Hooper for bouncing info off; Anne Feltham for loan of Bush Telegraph; Nigel Hall for his architectural walk around Totterdown; Shahzia Daya for tweezing out and getting info on the Unpaid Balances Fund, together with Mike Leigh of the Record Office; Guy Bristow for his birthday present of the 1902 map of Totterdown years ago which started all this off.

For history input
The immensely knowledgeable and helpful staff at Bristol Record Office, the University of Bristol Theatre Collection and Bristol Reference Library; also Bristol University for granting me Alumni access to their libraries.

Last but by no means least
Richard Jones for editing the first muddly MS, his support and for believing it was worth publishing and to Front Room, the Totterdown Art Trail, for providing an opportunity to air it publicly at a time when Totterdown is heaving with locals and visitors.

Preface by Gerry Brooke

As the place where my children first saw the light of day and where my family grew up throughout the 1970s and '80s, Totterdown, which picturesquely straddles the Bath and Wells Roads, will always rate highly in my affections. When, in 1977, we moved into our first home, a brick built Victorian terrace house in Hawthorne Street, with its back garden overlooking a wonderfully atmospheric Arnos Vale Cemetery, I never guessed that we would become embroiled in a last ditch fight over a long standing controversy – the Outer Circuit Road.

Passing up and down the Wells Road in the early 1970s I had been appalled to see the utter devastation caused by the destruction of hundreds of homes, pubs and shops to make way for a planned new super highway stretching from Easton, across St Philips Marsh and then ploughing on through Windmill Hill and Bedminster.

This heartless demolition had ripped the soul out of what had once been an extremely close knit community and many residents had become upset, depressed, and, not surprisingly, somewhat apathetic and resigned to their fate. By 1977 we thought, like many other people, that the intrusive road plans conceived in the 1960s had died a natural death. But then we discovered, to our horror, that there were still ambitions for major highway works here.

And so a group of like minded individuals – determined that Totterdown people shouldn't be steam rollered over yet again – decided to get together and form Totterdown Action Group with its catchy motto, later made into a badge, 'Build a Better Totterdown'.

How the unnecessary and over ambitious road plans was eventually toned down and new houses built where the old had once stood, is a story that you can learn about as you turn the pages of this book.

It was that long, hard, three-year fight that resulted in the rebirth of Victorian Totterdown – a charming, unique place which so many young people are today proud to call home.

Gerry Brooke
Editor of the *Evening Post*'s 'Bristol Times'

Introduction

Totterdown Rising is a book about a community that was split in half to make way for a road that was never built.

It's not a book about a community beaten into submission by a local council's obsession with the motor car, it's a story of how people rebuilt their community and reinvented the very special Spirit of Totterdown. But there is more to the story than a tale of a resurgent community. Kate Pollard's detailed research has uncovered some alarming facts about the role of the City Council in the demolition of Totterdown. It appears that the detailed plans to knock down an entire community, shops and pubs was never voted on and that the council pressed ahead with the demolition before they had received Government backing for the Road plan.

The Missing £43,000

In the course of researching this book, Kate Pollard also discovered that the houses that were demolished to make way for the Outer Circuit Road were the subject of compulsory purchase orders. In the case of a number of houses, the owners were absent and were not found within the timetable of the demolition process. In case they reappeared at a later date to discover their houses had gone, in around 1970 the Council lodged a fund in the 'Unclaimed Balances' section of the Chancery Courts in London so that some compensation

Wells Road, Bushy Park. The former Lloyds Bank is behind the trams, not yet become the YMCA.

could be administered to them. Through painstaking research and with some persistence Kate Pollard has tracked down that money and the revelation that the unclaimed balance of it should have been reclaimed by Bristol Council many years ago. (This is not an unusual situation. Many such funds lie dormant and are patiently tweezed out by funding researchers generations later.) In July 2006 Bristol City Council's Senior Solicitor (Corporate) confirmed that the money was still held at the Court Funds Office and by the end of the book we can report on the outcome to date.

The Good Guys and the Bad Guys Disclaimer

It became clear from the start of collecting information for this book that there were people involved in the story who were clearly those responsible for the rolling out of the Outer Circuit Road in Bristol irrespective of what or who was in its way. From the viewpoint of Totterdown people and their sympathizers, they were The Bad Guys, of course. There were also the key players at all levels in the story who did all they could to subvert the route of the planned road for the sake of Totterdown and communities further along it and others who set up, developed or fought for places and activities in Totterdown in order to bring some positive influences into the area. Obviously these are thought of as the Good Guys.

In retrospect it seems that there were people who were Good Guys at one time and place

Bath Road in 1969. The Turnpike pub (on the right) locates this former Bath Road terrace for you. (BEP)

'Easton – Bristol's largest comprehensive development area', from the 1966 Plan.

The Outer Circuit Road crossing re-developed Bedminster (note how it flys over Bedminster Bridge). From the 1966 Development Plan.

and Bad Guys at another; also that emotions ran high on all sides and that there were often more than two sides anyway. Time does not heal all wounds but retrospection is a wonderful thing! Many people who have contributed have astonished me by pointing out very understandingly the redeeming features of characters I had assumed would be their anti-heroes – and vice versa.

This is all a preamble leading up to saying that I have done the best I could with the memories and records that are available now – with some unsuppressible irony in places. If I have misunderstood or misinterpreted people's agendas, I apologise unreservedly. Hopefully no feelings of people still around will be hurt by what I've written.

Wally Jenkins and Gervas Walker

In the 60s, there were two city councillors who were enthusiasts for the private car and urban highway, Wally Jenkins (Labour) and Gervas Walker (Conservative) were of different political colours but shared startlingly similar opinions and a duality of council positions. A 1969 *Evening Post* article shows that at that date, Walker was Citizen Councillor of Stapleton. By 1972 Jenkins was Leader of the Council and Chair of the Planning and Traffic Committee and Walker was Shadow Chair. The two were politically close, wanted progress and provided continuity of tunnel vision in spite of political changes in the Council over the

The Outer Circuit Road was to cross the Floating Harbour. From the 1966 Development Plan.

years. Their shared view was that protesters were a thorn in the Planning Department's side. The spokespeople of Bristol's protest movement represented the public opinion that Jenkins and Walker were sceptical of and saw as a bar to progress. These protest people were indeed self-interested – particularly the Clifton lobby, which Jenkins and Walker both hated.

Between 1963 and 1973, both men were leaders of their parties. Jenkins (dubbed 'Mr Traffic' in the local press) was Deputy Leader for Labour between 1966–71 and also Chair or Shadow Chair of the Planning Committee. They were in strong positions to dictate policy and ensure political support and often consensus. In 1961 a newly established Traffic Engineering Section was set up in the Council to set out road plans. As it was single-interest, separate from both Planning and Engineering and responsible directly to the City Engineer, it created a powerful catalyst for road building proposals. The Planning Department was rarely consulted and played a very subordinate role (apart from over Cumberland Basin planning). The same year of its establishment, the Outer Circuit Road Plan was devised, based on 'data available' and local knowledge of road system deficiencies. It was an amalgam of schemes already on the Drawing board.

It would not be true to say that these men dragged unwilling councillors kicking and screaming behind them during the urban highway adventure. Those in both parties were in favour of Bristol's Outer Circuit Road from start to near the finish.

Pre-demolition Bath Road. On the left, the Bath Hotel, then Park Street. The Turnpike pub can just be picked out further along on the same side. (BEP)

The Three Lamps, 1965. (BEP)

1 Pre-Road Plan Totterdown

It used to be beautiful in Totterdown and I can still name the shops that were there. You could go into town to buy something and not be able to get it – but you could always get it in Totterdown. Kathleen Warren, formerly of Oxford Street

Until the time of the Road Plan, Totterdown had been full of specialist shops and stalls selling all manner of fresh food, haberdashery, fancy goods, newsagents' goods, leather goods, furnishings, building and DIY kit and so on. Totterdown people only needed to shop locally and other shoppers flocked in from elsewhere – from Knowle and Brislington, South Bristol and outside Bristol. Until the Beeching Cuts of the 1960s there were tremendous train links networked around the city. Totterdown was a well-known shopping centre for miles around. Locals reminiscing say that crowds of people arrived by train, later on bused in and even later came by car to shop in Totterdown rather than in Bristol's Broadmead shopping centre.

Pre-Road Totterdown has been photographically illustrated most beautifully in the Fishers' old postcard book, *Bygone Totterdown and Knowle* and also in *Knowle and Totterdown* by Mike Hooper et al.(1) The pictures show the densely packed shopping and residential area that older people still remember as 'Old Totterdown'. Shops and houses lined St Luke's Road, including on the Victoria Park side; on the Wells Road from below Three Lamps, and then above, tall shops stood on both sides. Where the grass and trees are landscaped on the right of the Wells Road and between St John's Lane and Oxford Street, there were once houses, businesses and shops, also in Cheapside. The west side of Bushy Park, now landscaped and enclosing the little park, and the sheltered housing, was the site of Totterdown's oldest buildings, cottages and businesses. Three storey shop buildings extended further up the Wells Road hill on both sides and beyond Firfield Road.

What is now called the Three Lamps Development was formerly densely terraced houses opening onto the pavements; below it on the Bath Road, lines of tall old buildings stood on both sides and included Victorian pubs and shops. North of the Bath Road is the river where even into the 1960s there was still very busy barge traffic and a shipwright's at Totterdown Bridge. Barges were frequently pulled up by tugs to be repaired there. This busy river life is well remembered by Mr and Mrs McCloud who kept the Bath Road newsagents' shop and Vivien Pipping whose family house overlooked the river at the rear. Overall, most of the commercial building lined the main roads whilst the houses were in side streets.

Landlocked in Totterdown, 1989. Possibly the last to dock in Totterdown were the South Family who were going to sail around the world. This former crane barge, Duchess, was the first step in a complicated list of ambitions. (BEP)

Totterdown as a shopping centre

Many of the following reminiscences date from the 1940s but in truth little of significance had changed between then and the pre-demolition era.

Brenda Spriggs confirmed that there was just such a range of shops in Totterdown – even a poodle parlour! They all specialised – you visited each shop for each thing. Kathleen Townsend remembered that when she lived in Oxford Street, 'at the back of us was the Chinese Laundry, managed by a Chinese man and his Welsh wife. They made the collars all nice and that. We got lots of steam. The neighbours complained a lot about that.' Mike Leigh of Bristol Record Office can also remember his parents taking their poodle to the poodle par-lor... 'but Dad learnt quite quickly and soon started cutting her himself. I can also remember Dad taking his shirt collars (they were detachable in those days) to the Chinese laundry – they always came back as stiff as a board'. The McClouds recalled that there was a Totterdown Undertakers, run by a woman, on the corner near Three Lamps.

One of the three-storeyed Bath Road shops – Number 100 – was Bushy TV. It stood between the former County Street and Angers Road turnings and was flanked by Cookes, the McClouds' News empire and the Haberdashers'. This was where Clive Clifford worked as a young apprentice. One of the partners, Mr Edwards, continued the business after the Road debacle, by moving to Green Street on Pylle Hill. Even this location was risky as no-one ever knew where the Road would go. The Pylle Hill area appears to have once been dotted with corner shops and had a pub and/or an off-licence on every corner. These had remained with the same family over generations. The emphasis was on the high quality of beer and its price rather than the comfort of the interior...bread, cheese and onions was the food most gener-ally offered. Clive recalls the garage on Angers Road which had to move to Hartcliffe, when the evictions were under way.

(i)1918 OS map of Totterdown, showing the pre-demolition layout of Bath Road and Middle Totterdown. (Ordnance Survey Office)

(ii) 1948 OS map of Totterdown showing the pre-demolition layout of the Belleview area. (Ordnance Survey Office)

(iii) 1918 OS map of Totterdown showing most of the original St Lukes Road and Oxford Street. (Ordnance Survey Office)

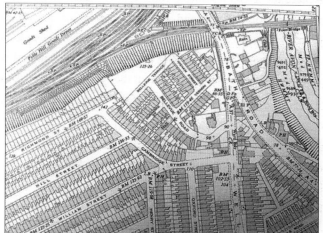

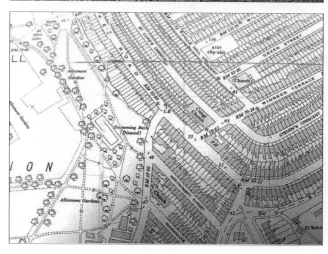

Totterdown entertainment (there were once working men's clubs, snooker, church clubs etc) was well catered for by Totterdown's own popular cinema, the Knowle Picture House, which stood on the site of the present Patco's. Opened in 1913, it had continued to operate, even through WW2 and despite the subsequent building of the Gaiety at Knowle by the same owner. After 50 years of being both 'The Flea Pit' and 'The Bug House' to Totterdown residents, in 1961, however, it closed because of the arrival of TV and dwindling audiences – not for the Road Plan. The Knowle Picture House, with an audience queue, is commemorated by a mural at the rear of the building, painted by Mark Courtney which was 'opened' by George Ferguson in 2005. The ornate, historic building was demolished to make way for a small supermarket – a Gateway. Mike Leigh of Bristol Record Office remembers it well and says: 'We (Mike and Madeline Leigh) even worked in the Gateway (which was the first shop to replace the 'Flea Pit') during 1962-3, after school on a Friday and on Saturday morning. We got 15s.0d for that time and looking back it seems that we could afford to do more with that than we can with our salaries today. Money seemed to get more for you in those days!'

Totterdown's busy shopping life was also remembered by Elsie Lawrance in her book which goes back to her childhood in the 1920s. (2) In 1979, long after her Totterdown house had been demolished, she first heard that Harris & Tozers – the Drapers – was about to

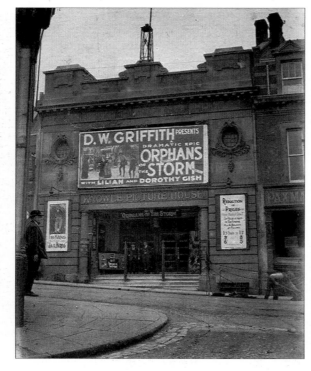

Frontage of the Knowle Picture House, on the site of the present Patco's store. (Denys Chamberlain)

close down. She writes: 'It was the last link in a long line of shops that had stretched from the Three Lamps to Firfield Street. The expense of the new fire precautions was doing to Harris & Tozers what the blitz of 1939-45 and the road planners of the 1960s had failed to do.'

She remembered how Harris & Tozers had struggled on with fewer and fewer customers as, one by one, the streets were demolished for the road scheme. Her grandmother, her mother then Elsie herself and then her children had all dealt there. Elsie's memories of Totterdown, with its daily shopping trips being part of routine community life, mirror all the older peoples' who still live here or once lived here or were evicted from here. In her childhood electric tramcars had clanged up and down the Wells Road every five minutes from the Red Lion Terminus to Bristol Bridge and to and from the Bath Road from Brislington Old Village to Hotwells.

By 1936 people were taking more and more to motorised traffic. Locally, motor-bikes were important to Totterdown life and were 'proven' on the Park Street hill, a source of great delight to local children – if they succeeded to get up the Vale Street hill as well, they would be rewarded with a cheer. It's hard to make out whether it was the presence of Totterdown's hills or the local personnel, but there was a Totterdown love affair with the motor-bike. Clive well recalls the iconic Glanfield Lawrence motorcycle shop near Bushy TV, where they worked on the racing bikes used by the famous Bristol Bulldogs which were tested out on Park Street. Knowle Speedway had a huge following in Totterdown. Brenda recalls

Mark Courtney's 2005 mural on the rear of and commemorating the Knowle Picture House, Winton Street. (Kate Pollard)

Denys Chamberlain, son of the original owner of the Picture House and the Gaiety, at the mural opening. (Kate Pollard)

Totterdown's Victorian post box, outside the present Tesco's, with Marge Dudbridge. Marge worked at the demolished post office in Shepherds, was evicted from her Angers Road home and later returned to work at the next Post Office, now Ali's Kebabs. 'Her cheerful grumpiness brightens my day' said a *My Bit of Bristol* feature writer. (BEP)

that her mother was an enthusiastic fan and that Mike Beddoe, who kept a corner shop selling motor bike bits, used to practice standing up on his bike and roared up and down Summer Hill where she lived.

The former Harris & Tozer building, described by Elsie is another Totterdown icon. It was bought from Harris and Tozers around 1979 by John Grimshaw – Civil Engineer and Bristol Protest network member – and Sue Learner and developed as 'The Totterdown Shopping and Community Centre' by them, supported by other community members to give Totterdown back some of the shopping facilities and community life so recently lost. They set up the Children's Workshop (still there), ran courses and community development and repair schemes; the seeds of future cycle paths planning were cultivated there. The original Harris and Tozers shop is also remembered affectionately by many Totterdown elders who still recall that the shop allowed corsets to be taken home on approval – by them as children – for Grandmother to try on. This anecdote encapsulates those days – corsets, trusting shopkeepers and unembarrassed youngsters being sent out on family shopping missions!

Other shops were also to be found in every Totterdown side street, together with a formidable number of pubs and off licences. Extending as they did along both sides of the Bath Road and the Wells Road from Three Lamps, young Elsie Lawrance, growing up in her street in 'Middle Totterdown' would be told: 'On with your coat, we are going up top' (Wells Road), or it could be 'down the bottom' on Bath Road. Ascending by way of Parliament Street, Hillside Terrace and Highgrove Street to 'up top' brought them out midway in the shopping area. This is where Harris and Tozers competition, Greenough's Drapery, was, where they would buy the necessary overalls and stockings. On the main road were the big shops – the Home & Colonial, Co-op, David Greig's and Kings. Lower down was the Maypole, and on the corner of Cheapside was Seasons: the aristocrat of grocery shops, dealing with the more superior customers.

The original Harris and Tozers. (BEP) 'Now there was a shop. Everything in the haberdashery line you could think of'.

Elsie particularly liked Flooks the Butchers with its china stands of roast leg of pork, silverside of beef, pressed beef, ham on the bone and tongue. The delicacies of the time, black puddings and polonies would be looped up in the window and there would be dishes of pigs' trotters and Bath chaps ready to eat. There were no end of butchers' shops to choose from – Cooks on Bath Road then on or near the Wells Road, Harris's (originally in School Road) and Humphreys, Parsons, Eastmans, Slaters in Cheapside, and Tihorns. Clive also remembers a meat warehouse operating next to his Edwards TV shop in Green Street, Pylle Hill. Totterdown was well supplied with fish as well as meat. Brenda Spriggs speaks enthusiastically about Totterdown's many fish and chip shops, especially one on the Bath Road and calculates that there were also three wet fish shops.

At the top of (the original) New Walls Road was (it seemed to Elsie) an Aladdin's Cave of a shop – Fansons Hardware Shop which stocked everything – hardware and tools, cooking ware, cleaning stuffs and in her early days Elsie would see ranks of the absolute necessity of the time, chamber pots tailored to suit all ages and posterior sizes. Close by, on the corner of (the former) Angers Road and Bath Road was another hardware shop much loved by Elsie which sold cat meat – and more importantly, rather desirable celluloid dolls.

Home sewing, mending and dressmaking were the norm in those days, and there were also professional needlewomen and seamstresses in Totterdown. One of the latter was remembered by Vivien Pipping; she lived and worked in an old cottage in the road behind the original Bush Hotel – roughly where the little park beside the old YMCA building now is. They were provided with all the necessary sewing items by the many other drapery shops in the district, including the Misses Wathen, whose haberdashery was at the top of (the former) County Street. A gentlemen's outfitters, Burridges, catered for the men. The big and bigger shops lined the main roads and in all the side streets wrote Elsie where little corner

The Blue Bowl Inn near Three Lamps backing onto the river. Its basement bowling alley was flooded at high tide, remembers Jim Dudbridge. (BEP)

shops, amongst the houses. This was the Totterdown remembered now only by its older residents; some are still here; many were evicted, some moved on and some have passed on. This book is a homage to all those people; I have tried to reconstruct 'what happened to Totterdown' in that very different era and to celebrate the work of the many activists and movers and shakers who tried to stop the Road and/or make things better for the people who were left amid the desolation. Brenda has pointed out that, by the time of the Road: 'It wasn't only a case of what was closed down but – even at a distance – what went out of business. The people were taken away and the shops then had no business!'

The Road Plan isn't to blame for every change that has taken place in Totterdown – it just made it happen more painfully and in one fell swoop. In fact, the local authority spokespeople publicly justified the road building era because of the social changes that were taking place, including the new shopping trends. The 1960s upsurge of convenience food, fridges and freezer boxes, labour-saving devices and promises of future increased leisure time – and the car of course – were bringing in changes in consciousness. (Clive thinks shopping changes had already started in Lower Totterdown around 1970 when the first Oxford Street shops customer was spotted coming past with a Tesco bag, defiantly stating that 'it was cheaper down there!')

How many labour-saving devices had penetrated Totterdown at this time and whether increased leisure was being enjoyed here is hard to say. What is certain is that in many other places these were more gradual changes. In Totterdown and other similarly affected areas, the former pattern of life was rapidly and radically swept away, making it impossible for people caught up in it on both a psychological and practical level.

By the end of the demolition period, there were few shops for staple food left in Totterdown. There were a few corner shop/newsagents, notably on the Bath Road (though these were to close eventually too) and there was Frank Smith's Off Licence in William Street. Given the number of elderly people and Totterdown's gradient, the wholefoods and other 'stalls' in the Totterdown Centre were a welcome and accessibly placed addition. In the specialist businesses described above, friendly personal service had been the norm; shops had been meeting places, where people had time to stop and have conversations. Totterdown was very much a village community in that respect, in the same way that, further east on the road's route, Barton Hill had also once enjoyed its own village life. Brenda remembers when every street in Totterdown had a corner shop where people called in for news and a chat which was of course a part of the national pattern at that time.

The bath Tavern stood next to metal fabrication works just the station side of Bath Bridge. (BEP)

The 'Unpaid Balances Fund'

I have attempted to place Totterdown's 'Brave New World' experiences into the context of those years and to research the whole story as it unfolded from as many different angles as I could. Part of that was to make a lengthy trawl through some of the Council Minutes Books of the time. I am most grateful to the staff at Bristol's Record Office and Modern Records for all the help and support they gave me over this. It was at this stage that I was became aware that when compulsory purchase orders, valuation and compensation procedures were being negotiated between the Council and the people on the ground in Totterdown in extreme haste, a number of Totterdown house owners did not respond to their official letters. In the absence of replies and compliance from them and from freehold and leasehold landowners, compulsory purchase orders were fruitlessly delivered, eviction orders were made to deaf ears and houses were demolished anyway.

One can only guess why there were absentee house owners. There were many generations of affected Totterdown people and some were elderly. Some reminiscers say that many became ill and died because of the strain. In 1973 a GP writing in the *Evening Post* cited patients in the Victoria Park and Bedminster area whom he said literally hoped to die before this happens (ie their houses were knocked down). As the Societies and Charities existing to trace missing people know too well, individuals do frequently disappear without trace or apparent reason. One could also conjecture that other owners did not hold the necessary ownership papers; yet others may have moved elsewhere or even abroad. In case these people ever reappeared, in around 1970 the Council placed a fund in Chancery with which returning owners could be reimbursed – if they could provide copper bottomed proof of

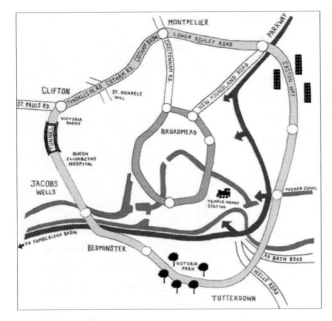

On December 15, 1966 the Ministry of Transport approved a Bristol City Council plan for a £30 million Outer Circuit Road.

This map is based on an illustration that appeared in the *Evening Post* on Friday October 15, 1971. The black line shows the route proposed by *Evening Post* reader Paul Chadd which would have taken traffic through a largely derelict area of St Philip and would have followed the Avon along York Road. The grey line is the route preferred by the City Council. Much of Easton was demolished to make way for the first stage of the road, which is now called Easton Way. In 1972 the middle part of Totterdown was largely demolished to make way for the road which was never built. Note the route of the four-lane highway after leaving Totterdown – across Victoria Park, round the back of the Cathedral, a tunnel underneath Brandon Hill and a dual carriageway through the heart of Cotham and Montpelier. Thanks to the *Naked Guide to Bristol* for the use of the illustration.

ownership. In the interests of adding the outcome of this action into this account of Totterdown's history, I looked for the continuing existence of the fund early in 2005 and eventually discovered the appropriate Council department to talk about it. The prospect for a researcher of discovering how many owners were affected, how many traced, how many were never located, was, I thought, of interest to the overall history. I also asked if, should the fund be located and returned to Bristol, some of it could be ring-fenced for use in Totterdown. Quartet (formerly the Greater Bristol Foundation), agreed to administer any such funds if called on to do so.

By the time the book is ready for publishing in Totterdown we hope to be able to report on the outcome and maybe add some details of how many and when the beneficiaries reappeared, so we will revisit this story at the end of the book.

2 Totterdown and the Motorway Age

These people had been through two wars and thought that all would be well from then on.
Clive Clifford, former Edwards TV Manager, Green Street

When Gervas Walker publicly announced the Outer Circuit Road Scheme Totterdown suddenly discovered that it was in the way of a big urban highway road plan that it had previously heard nothing about, known as the Bristol Outer Circuit Road. It was to start out in South East Bristol's Lawrence Hill, as an urban continuation of the nearly completed M32 which was about to enter the city via a part-elevated stretch called the Parkway. This was to run, surreally, on the same level as the bedroom windows of its neighbouring Eastville houses and into Montpelier and was to be built to funnel the new M5 traffic from South Wales, the Southwest, the Midlands and London into Bristol, for the first time. Lawrence Hill had long been declared an Action Area in which demolition and re-housing were taking place so compulsory purchase and land acquisition was in full swing and 1960s tower block housing not far behind.

The Outer Circuit Road was then to travel westwards, bridge the river at St Philips and then cut a swathe through the middle of Totterdown, cause the demolition of other areas, (eg Bedminster and Southville), tunnel under immovable obstacles, (eg Brandon Hill), fly over the more prestigious sites, (Clifton, the river, Cotham and the University campus) and then re-join the Parkway via another swathe cut through Montpelier;(1) it was designed to circle Bristol at a three-quarter mile distance from the city centre.

At its Stage 3, in Totterdown, it would ascend a four-level highway interchange at Three Lamps Junction. At this early point no-one in Totterdown had yet visualised what the actual breadth of a two-lanes-each-way urban highway would be like, or the area, height and depth of a four-level interchange; or even that the surrounding perimeter of land would also be required for operational equipment, outgoing soil and incoming materials and the subsequent construction of safety barriers and landscaping. The interchange center, as it was called, was to be one of several along the route of the road. The Three Lamps one would be reached via an extra highway lane to Wells Road and a slip road from Bath Road East. Freeman Fox's plan also included pedestrian and cycleways.

In 1972 the term Transportation Interchange Centre was first described as:

> A large multi-storey car park, to which access could be obtained from a number of points around the complex at various levels and the whole to be combined with a bus

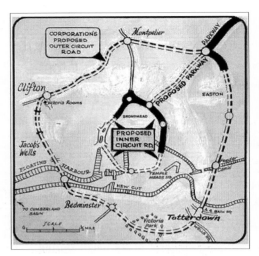

The projected Outer Circuit Road route. (BEP)

station...to enable drivers to leave their cars outside the congested areas of Bristol's center and main shopping area and to carry on by bus...at least the site is intended for this possibility, a fact which those in the next era may be truly thankful.

This was in an article: 'Bristol's Outer Circuit Road by a Citizen', in *Bristol Illustrated*, April 1972. The model and the drawn plans of the time showed the Road rather than what or who was in its way. The civil engineers' plans for their work and for Council reference, which are drawn directly over the map of the city's streets, show the Road's route. At first sight it looks as though the Civil Engineer's drawing office had run out of paper and been forced to use old maps as a substitute. (2) The eventual outcome was that during Totterdown's demolition years beginning in 1968, 550 Totterdown houses and businesses would be demolished and around 2,000 local people evicted even before the proposed road had reached a final draft and been funded. It was a localised crisis which provided Totterdown with its Wilderness Years. These were to linger way beyond the eventual cancellation of these extreme road schemes and the rehabilitation when a line could be drawn under the redevelopment of Totterdown – but they were by no means unique to Totterdown. Many cities throughout the country were having parallel experiences and it is interesting – and depressing in equal measures – to fit the Lawrence Hill and Totterdown stories into the national planning context.

The urban highway age

In the post-war decades there had been an ethos of optimism, new freedoms and the replacement of aged, outdated and overcrowded housing which was believed to have caused the epidemics of the past. The post-war rebuilding programme was carried out in haste but as further 'Brave New World' development followed in its wake, it became clear that for people in both the less and more privileged localities that were directly affected, there was an acceptance threshold that could and would be reached that was well below the level of enthusiasm for development shared by the planners of both central and local government. In Totterdown the urban highway age was characterised by non-communication on any meaningful level between the local authority and people, stoked by massive delays in publishing reports which affected the lives of residents, and lack of information. This was partly to do with local authority indecision and secrecy, and partly to do with lack of information on the ground where there were frightened people – a recipe for assumptions and conspiracy theory.

Freeman Fox's Proposal for the Outer Circuit Road's configuration north of Totterdown Bridge. They were the designers of the Cumberland Basin – see the similarity.

By the end of the 1950s, central government was working to accelerate economic growth; it had also seen the proliferation of car ownership and wanted to encourage this because car ownership was intrinsic to growth. In 1963, Tony Benn, MP for South East Bristol, (which then included Totterdown), had pointed out that between 1952 and 1959, the Tories had built six inches of new road for every new vehicle that came off the production line and that in the developed world, car production figures had become the prime index for measuring economic growth. In 1963 Benn characterized the ideological struggle between capitalism and communism as a straight fight between Henry Ford and Karl Marx. Marx's vision of the collectivist state were challenged by Ford's mass produced motor cars – symbol of affluence in capitalist societies wooing the workers from their class loyalties and destroying socialism for all time. Henry Ford's motors had 'made the world safe for a car-owning democracy and free enterprise'. (3) Growth meant modernisation on a national scale; modernisation meant more public spending on science and technology, on a revitalized regional infrastructure and by no means least, on slum clearance and reshaping the city around the motor car. Government also believed that unmanageable traffic congestion in city centres was imminent, with soaring numbers of road accidents, which Benn had also pointed to. In 1963 there had been nearly 7,000 fatalities, 90,000 serious injuries and 250,000 less serious, Benn wrote, and the age of safer driving campaigns began. (4)

The Minister of Housing Sir Keith Joseph commented that urban renewal and road development with the right policies could be tackled simultaneously; (5) this was demonstrated in Bristol's Lawrence Hill Action Area. In 1960, Joseph had appointed Colin Buchanan to make a study of the long-term development of traffic in urban areas. Buchanan's work not

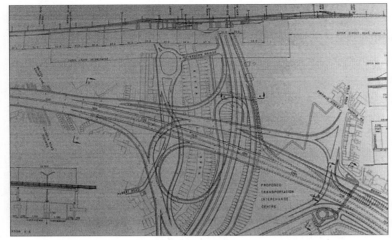

Freeman Fox's Outer Circuit
Road Proposal Plan,
Totterdown section.
Locate yourself via
Totterdown Bridge,
centre top.

only informed all subsequent road and transport planning but it also leant very heavily on
North American planning theory.

Up to the 1960s local authority development plans were dominated by proposals for large
radial and inner ring roads of motorway standard for cities. Until the mid 1960s the need for
these urban motorways had been generally accepted and supported by the general public.
(6) In fact the media had joined in with their own proposals. (7) At the time it was felt that
a crisis of urban traffic congestion was imminent because traffic was forecast to grow very
rapidly in the years ahead. Cars got larger by an average three inches each between 1961-74
and faster by 14mph between 1974 and 1961. (8) Economic forces were actually fashioning
cars to create street congestion and after Buchanan there was a general acceptance that uni-
versal car ownership was a real probability.

In the late 1960s and although traffic constraints in cities was mooted, the road programme continued and the Government aimed to build 1000 miles of inter city motorways
as an improvement on the former 'trunk road' network for carrying lorries and goods and
then to divert road budgets to urban highway construction in towns. Consequently in 1964
'each community would have to decide for itself where it stood in relation...to the trade-off
between accessibility and the environment'. (9) This was the point at which the concept of
'the new type of transport surveys' was born – the Land Use and Transport Survey, (LUTS),
another method imported from North America.

With hindsight it is known that the traffic growth predictions were wildly inaccurate and
LUTS surveys in many cases were too insensitively applied. Often they were used to confirm
plans already on the drawing board. It seems as if the politicians' desire for fast economic

growth became subconsciously self-fulfilled by the surveys. The government encouraged, supported and subsidised LUTS. Many cities began their LUTS surveys in the 60s; Bristol's waited until the 1970s and it may have benefited by the delay into another decade. (10)

The beginnings of protest

Among ordinary people those tolerance thresholds in respect of extreme neighbourhood alterations had already been reached; Buchanan's twin two-lane motorway tunnel under central Bath led to furious debate in 1966 and there was angry controversy over a new inner ring road in Oxford. In 1966, as well, on the day following the opening of the M4 viaduct, London people saw press images of sections of the London Road Plans for the first time. Adverse headlines began to appear, e.g. the *London Standard*: 'Group fights premature London motorway plan'.

Very soon a national anti-motorway campaign was in full swing, supported by the press. The *Times* Transport Correspondent pointed out that motorways had become 'a focus for fear' because of house clearances and because people also had to live in close proximity with motorways (as had happened in Eastville), causing not only supreme inconvenience but death to house-selling. (11) Other similarly affected cities in 1968, the year in which Totterdown demolition began, were Portsmouth and Southampton and closer to home, Cardiff, whose council had planned 24 miles of urban motorway-standard road with a 6-mile concreted area including flyovers and unders requiring the land beneath 1,500 homes. Although the Cardiff press was pro-road, there was a powerful opposition lobby. (12)

In the 1960s, opposition was localised but the early signs were there for central government to read. It will be clear later that the Bristol Council had to confer with central Government regularly because of the opposition to the Bristol Outer Circuit Road and Totterdown. It will also be clear that Governmental post-war growth and renewal policies devolved down to local authorities – Bristol's included – and that urban highway building policy was central to it.

Following the war, the Government had been concerned to update legislation to deal with what it saw as the demands of new situations. Britain was more densely populated and wealthier and its people had more cars and more leisure time than in the 1940s, so the nature of the demand for land had changed considerably. To enable land to be acquired and developed in line with Government policy, an updated new Town and Country Planning Act was put in place in 1967 and its purpose was: 'To provide pleasant surroundings for people to live and work in'. It aimed to strike a balance between claims on land by homes, industry, transport and leisure. It also gave local authorities the right to compulsorily purchase.

One fell swoop –
Totterdown in
pieces after 1968.

When the lists of evictees from Totterdown began to appear in Council minutes from
1968, they were noted – as were all actions under the appropriate legislative heading –
under Town and Country Planning Act. Presumably this was about precise record keeping
but also of course it justified the actions as compliance with Government orders. In Bristol,
urban highway planning was a microcosm of what was happening nationally when in 1966
Bristol – and Totterdown – first heard officially about the plan which would alter many lives
across the South East side of the city. It was publicised in the local press, in *Civic News*, in
Bristol Illustrated and demonstrated in a model at Quakers Friars. (13) By today's standard
this would not be considered adequate, targeted information dissemination but at that time
public consultation had not been made a legal requirement. *Bristol Illustrated* was a society
gossip magazine, unlikely to be read outside of Bristol's areas of privilege. However, in this
case, Clifton and Cotham would also be affected. The information was very startling and very
general – there were no specifics in terms of actual locations or areas which would be cleared.

What happened in Totterdown

Vivien Pipping and family lived on the Bath Road before compulsory purchase began there.
She remembers the day her letter arrived to explain that their house had to go to make way
for the Road improvement. She had barely had time to digest it before her neighbours 'in the
side roads' arrived at her door with theirs also in their hands.

Vivien was well-known in Totterdown and had attributes which drew people to her for advice. The neighbours, Vivien remembers, were very distraught. Everyone had a deadline by which to get their houses valued. Vivien gave them what support she could and recalls that her house became an unofficial advice centre over that period as there seemed no other source of information was available. She told them what no-one else did – that they would be able to get their houses valued independently and claim moving expenses; and that they had time to consider the situation thoroughly. (14)

Apart from the compulsory purchase orders arriving out of the blue, Totterdown appears to have been an information-free zone. Vivien, a well-educated, community-orientated and politically aware individual who would have noticed, remembers that: 'Totterdown people were given no information from start to finish – except leaflets given out at public meetings' – (which were usually held in response to public demand); but it has to be said that it'd be a hard job to display local posters explaining:

> We're going to evict the residents of X number of Totterdown streets almost immediately (though we reserve the right to keep changing our minds about which ones), pull their houses down and replace them by a four-level highway interchange. Sorry, everyone!

The demolition process started in 1968. The 'core site' being prepared for Road construction was roughly a quarter of Totterdown, comprising firstly the section of land right in its centre, containing ten internal streets with dwellings, corner shops and off-licences and bounded by the main Bath and Wells Roads which were lined with the businesses which comprised most of Totterdown's shopping centre. This would provide the land on which to construct the four-level highway interchange on which to redirect the incoming and outgoing motorway traffic to and from the city.

Arriving from the east, the rising highway leading up to it would have arrived in Totterdown from the river and two rows of tall houses, Victorian pubs and businesses lining Bath Road were demolished there. An area between the west side of Bushy Park and Victoria Park was also affected. The highway was then to bisect Victoria Park, and run through Bedminster and Southville. However, the plan for Totterdown's part of the route periodically changed so that houses were semi-demolished, then were rebuilt, then finally demolished completely before that part of the plan was eventually scrapped altogether. (15)

What Bath Road looked like after 1974. (EP)

Sidney Gill, Grocer, outside his St Luke's Road shop – the only remaining one. (BEP)

3   Compulsory Purchase in Totterdown

When the Development Map came out with grey and pink areas, Highgrove Street was
pink and therefore was due to disappear under the Outer Circuit Road.
David Cox, who formerly lived on Highgrove Street where his grandparents and then his
parents had lived before him.

Nonone of the reminiscing evictees now remembers how soon after 1966 they received
orders to vacate their homes to make way for 'road improvements', together with an
explanation of the powers of compulsory purchase. But they do recall that they were advised
to contact their solicitors and to be ready to negotiate a house price with the City Valuer.

The McClouds who ran the newsagents on Bath Rd, remember that none of the people
they spoke to (which was many, on a day to day basis) actually *had* solicitors and they
believed that most families in Totterdown had lived there for generations since the houses
were built. Many were elderly, and a move for them to a strange part of the city was a massive
upheaval for which they were completely unwilling and unprepared and which some
elderly people didn't survive, the McClouds believe.

The land acquisition was managed by the Council's Planning and Traffic Committee
between 1968 and 1972. (1) As each section of the Outer Circuit Road was approved, the
Committee was authorised to negotiate for the 'additional lands' required. The finance
involved included the legal costs incurred in terms of negotiating a selling price with the
owner and compensation for moving or for business loss and these were low or minimal
because by this time Totterdown houses were unsellable on the open market; the Council
notes this is its Minutes and adds 'Properties which are considered should be acquired on
grounds of hardship'. For this reason, owners were forced to serve Blight Notices on the
Council with more legal costs to both sides, in order to win compensation fixed by the City
Valuer. 'Blighted' is a legal term.

The Council was pre-empting the arrival in Totterdown of the Outer Circuit Road by several
years, and the compulsorily purchasees were at first forced to put their houses on the
open market, if only to value them. Only someone who had arrived in Bristol from Mars
would be unaware of the road proposals by this stage, particularly because by 1969 there
were already empty and boarded up houses and demolition sites in Totterdown.
Consequently not only was it impossible to sell but the value of the houses was nil. There was
little or no precise information 'on the ground' in Totterdown but there was frequent news
items in the press of the Road's changes of route; no-one in Totterdown knew exactly where

it was going and for lengthy periods, the Council itself was undecided. The situation was frighteningly surreal; the route might go anywhere any time and who would want to come to live anywhere in an area where such dire things were happening? The whole of Totterdown was given a wide berth by purchasers. (2)

Blight was a circular and debilitating condition; people couldn't leave if they wanted to; everyone in such a close community felt wretched about the evictees, frightened that they might suddenly join their ranks, worried that there was nowhere to shop now and depressed about the prospect of living in close proximity to a four-level highway interchange and their shortly-to-be-decimated park.

The Council's house and land acquisition was piecemeal. In May 1968 houses were being purchased on St Luke's Road, Bath Road and on the Core Site, Angers and New Walls Roads and also on Bushy Park. Bristol Council went ahead in anticipation of acquiring Government funding for the highway; Compulsory Purchase and demolition continued. Houses were boarded up when they were vacated, were a target for vandalism and theft and had to be either demolished quickly or, as they were now Council-owned, re-let by the Council. Demolition was also continuing apace in the east of the city because of the fast approaching Parkway link to the motorway. The Victorian terraces of Pennywell Road were disappearing fast with Beam and Amberley Streets not far behind. Once in possession of a building, the Council could relax as the need to demolish, apart from avoiding vandalism, was not imminent and in some cases they could charge a rent. Vivien Pipping's family had been evicted from their newly DIYed Bath Road home and had in fact moved up the hill to a house on the east – and safe – side of nearby Bushy Park. They were therefore in a position to observe their former house being redecorated, let out to tenants for a considerable period and eventually the eviction of the tenants.

Another example was Oxford Street, where demolition had begun on the houses. There was a moratorium when the planned highway route was altered; the houses were repaired, had their roofs replaced and then were let to tenants for a while until after another change of plan, the houses were all finally demolished. This incident was called by the locals 'Oxford Street Stop and Go'. Numbers 8-10 Angers Road, the Totterdown Men's Adult School, were compulsorily purchased for £1,880. However the School itself had already closed down in 1968 after 60 years of use. Described by the *Evening Post* as the former Mecca of Totterdown engine drivers and shopkeepers it could no longer afford the rent. The Council then let out to a group of Social Work students who re-opened it as a youth club 'to take Totterdown children off the street into some kind of controlled environment – all children regardless of behavioural problems – and engage them in free activities'. It was open four evenings a week and all day on Saturdays. Lofty aims aside, it was evidently a thorn in the flesh for the remaining neighbours who complained bitterly through a 42-signature petition to the Council that the Club generated 'the maximum din' through its now glass-free windows. (3)

The Council took the side of the Club to which they gave freedom of tenancy until 1972, the date at which the highway was due to arrive in Totterdown, in order that the Club could qualify for a grant from the National Playing Fields Association.

The Council Minutes books itemised the evictees with whom they were legally involved over compensation and noted its difficulties over houses whose owners were not to be found.

The Attwells' home at the former Bushey Lodge, with marble lions (the Attwells' archives)

Some local eviction stories

Amongst the reminiscences there are some interesting, though sad, histories. Not all the houses demolished were Victorian artisan terraces. In Bushy Park there were a number of large and older houses and cottages. One was Bushey Lodge, (the older spelling of the road), at 66 Bushy Park on its south west side then owned by Reginald Attwell and family. Their considerable, stone built house was on four storeys at the rear and two on the Bushy Park

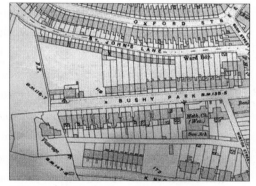

OS map showing the Attwells' and other imposing houses on Bushy Park.(Ordnance Survey office/BRO)

frontage, because of the slope. Its large garden already had a line of garages at the St John's Lane end, several former cottages and stables.

Mr Attwell ran a newspaper delivery business from the house and was also in the process of converting flats to let in it. He had successfully applied for planning permission for more lock-up garages and a filling station (the tanks were already installed in the garden) at the St John's Road end of the garden and intended the garden cottages to be for his children and their families.

The ghostly former Anstee home and business behind the Bush Hotel on Bushy Park, demolished with the rest. (BRO)

Attwell's children had grown up in Bushey Lodge and Mr Attwell was a creative thinker and inventor, and small business entrepreneur. These plans were well under way in 1966 and upon them depended Mr Attwell's ability to retire with a pension from work in his sixties with his family around him. The demand for his land for the highway ended this dream. Mr Attwell decided to fight the Council for fairer compensation and took it to court, acting as his own solicitor. He had had 66 Bushey Park valued independently some time before, demonstrated this and won a settlement of £11k for his property, his land and two vehicular rights of way over the adjoining land. This was not as good as it sounds because he lost a significant percentage of this in the Betterment Tax payable if the land was improved.

The family left, taking the bell which had been on the roof and the marble lions from the gateposts, which they still have in the family. Mr Attwell had to start up another newspaper selling business and worked hard for much of his curtailed retirement years elsewhere.

The other significant houses in Bushy Park where trade was also lost belonged to the Anstees, builders, who owned three houses in Bushy Grove directly behind the former Bush Hotel and a shop front on the Wells Road; also a 'very old cottage' occupied by a needle-woman remembered by Vivien Pipping. The Bush Hotel and the Westminster Bank fronting the Wells Road, Bushy Park side were demolished as was the Totterdown Hotel on the opposite side. (5)

The Council only re-sited larger, more vociferous businesses; numerous people lost their small businesses along with their homes and consequentially their livelihoods if they were unable to set up in another area.

Here are just a few of them: Mr French at 171 Bath Road who no longer had the business he had run there and was in bad health; AJ Jones of 17 Stanley Hill and Mrs Caddick of 101 Bath Road, had both suffered 'disturbance of trade'; shortly afterwards the Greengrocers at 82 Bath Road, a Grocer at 72 Wells Road, and the Confectioner at 92 Wells Road were awarded small compensations. Other businesses snuffed out were 21 and 41 County Street, 31 New Walls and 19 Stanley Hill. The Council agreed to buy the Swan pub on Bath Road and to rehouse its owner. AW Wilson was paid £300 as part payment for trade disturbance.

Other settlements went to Mills & Allen on Bath Road and the Midland Bank at 1 Bush St.

One luckier person was Clive Clifford – an old hand as an evictee, as his family had actually been compulsorily purchased and moved twice previously from other Bristol areas. By now he was a young man working for the Bushy TV partners whose shop was on Bath Road. The core of their business was in Totterdown and all would have been lost if they had moved the shop elsewhere. The move split the partners apart. One of them took retirement; the other moved the shop and took Clive with it to Green Street. There was obviously a risk of being evicted from there, too, but a move there was the only possible way to save the established local business. Even so it had to be built up again; TV rental came in at about this time, which helped to save it, plus the advent of colour TV and BBC2, Clive thinks.

Last remains of the Parkers' Bakery on the corner of Wells Road and Highgrove Street – the edge of Zone A. (BEP)

He is also sure that because of its strategic but even so, risky move, Edwards TV was one of the very few Totterdown businesses to survive. The Pipping's photography business also survived because they had been able to move to another part of Totterdown.

Houses at 8 Highgrove Street, and 8, 26 and 36 County Street were also emptied and at least five out of eight evictees in this last group were members of Totterdown's newly arrived Asian community. All these evictions were still two years ahead of the road's arrival in Totterdown – if it were to be approved. By May 1970, a major eviction year, no modification to the highway plan had been proposed so it seemed that the evictions would continue in Totterdown, though the road's passage through Bedminster via Victoria Park still required approval. This had to be published 'in the normal way' allowing 21 days for objections. This was the cause of the demolition of the row of St Luke's Road houses backing on to Victoria Park.

There was also a row of houses taken out on the Pylle Hill side of St Luke's Road. Local reminiscers say that this was because there was a Council mistake caused by a changed house number, (no. 13 becoming 12a for superstitious reasons at the end of the opposite terrace) and the Pylle Hill terrace was removed instead. Whatever the truth of this, this 200 yard terrace had been demolished in 1962, four years before the Road Development Plan and for earlier road widening scheme and this is dated by an *Evening Post* article and photograph in 1963. This reported that by that date the rubble had been left untouched for more than a year. Mrs Vi Paddick of the former 9 St Luke's Road claimed in the *Evening Post* in February 1963 that her mother had owned four houses there and was still paying ground rent for them. There is no written information to substantiate or disprove the superstition story but four evacuees, including one from St Luke's Road, tell the same story. It could be an urban myth but on the other hand, it could be a true story pre-dating the Outer Circuit Road demolition. Marilyn Webb had lived in the 1962-demolished terrace and recalls that she had been ordered to pay for her own house to be demolished – the only example of this yet discovered in Totterdown. This had once been a standard practice which may have still been prevalent in 1962. (6)

In the same year, Bristol's Housing Committee resolved to play its part to the best of its ability 'regarding the re-housing of the families to be displaced from this area'. The reality was that many of the families owned their own houses and also in many cases, businesses on the same site and were re-housed on new Council estates. Kathleen Warren and Anne Townsend's reminiscences show that some went to Stockwood which was then under construction.

Mrs Kathleen Warren, once an Oxford Street resident who now lives in sheltered housing in Stockwood, reported that some of her former neighbours from Totterdown had been living in Stockwood since their evictions. The McClouds' neighbours also went to Stockwood. In 1972, 161 homes were reportedly to be built for Totterdown evictees on Hengrove Farm, Clatworthy Drive and Airport Road, Whitchurch. They were to include several blocks of 'handicapped persons dwellings and OAP accommodation' near handy shops, buses, pubs and a new primary school. (7)

Mrs McCloud remembers her family's eviction from both their home and their family newsagents business on Bath Road. They believed there was no other choice and bought a house in St Anne's so as not to become homeless. A sympathetic Council Officer tried to persuade them to give it up and accept an interim council house, which move, he said, would be a better investment but his advice came too late. In 1972 more notices to businesses to quit were delivered on the Wells Road.

The payments made to evictees were disparate and without background information it is impossible to pinpoint the reasons for this. Totterdown people complained that the Council was offering them only 50 per cent of the market value of their houses and Conservative candidate-in-waiting Councillor Norman Reece advised evictees to consult the Land Tribunal before accepting any compensation offers. (8)

St Luke's Road
terrace backing
Victoria Park
demolished.
(Nigel Hall)

How it was
replaced.
(Kate Pollard)

Disparities may be part due to some people having been tougher at bargaining or some national businesses wielding more power. Bata Shoes, an old Bristol business, for example, received £5,000 'disturbance compensation' and the South West Electricity Board received £5,750. Mills and Allen at 31, 37 and 39 Bath Road received its final settlement in 1972 after 3-years of negotiation. Occasionally a business managed to get re-sited – for example T. Broad and Sons on 1-3 New Walls Road was granted a lease until 1982 of part of Cox's Yard in Montpelier.

The Outer Circuit Road plan was affecting Montpelier too, and the City Engineer assured worried people there that their section of the road 'would not be built within the next fifteen years' which accords with Broads' lease date. (9) At least evictees, as a rule, received some

The Three Lamps Signpost in storage at the Council's Dovercourt Road Depot. (Pat and Peter Wright)

compensation, if meagre. Clive Clifford's reminiscences of his family's earlier demolition history elsewhere in Bristol suggests that in other places at other times, compensation had not been forthcoming and that an evictee had been ordered to pay their own demolition fees.

In 1972, Totterdown's Three Lamps sign, held in great affection, was removed to Council Storage at Dovercourt Road, from which it would reappear in 1983, after thirteen year's exile and where it would presumably would have stayed had the interchange been built. It was visited every year by the local Councillor to check on its condition. (10)

Land acquisition and demolition continued through 1971 and at the same time, work on the Outer Circuit Road, Stage 1 at Lawrence Hill, had begun. Bristol City Council excused the wholesale demolition there with the explanation that the 100-year-old houses were due for replacement anyway. (11)

A rather large hole appeared where parts of Pennywell Road, Newfoundland Road and Mina Roads had once been and where the two-level interchange was to be constructed. The press pictures of this would have informed Totterdown people about the size of hole which would be required for one twice as large. (12) The *Bristol Evening Post* reported that Easton people re-housed in new tower blocks were living in close proximity to this hole on terrain which resembled a moonscape and generated dust and noise. (13)

In 1973, when the first stretch of the Outer Circuit Road was opened to traffic, there were in the region of 900 complaints from Lawrence Hill people about the new traffic noise levels. By then, five years after demolition in Totterdown was begun, the Government approved the whole Outer Circuit Road in principle and it then seemed certain that after 1973, Stage 2 would bring it to Totterdown. In early anticipation of that, Blight Notices were being served on the Council from Bedminster and Southville, anticipating the Road's next phase.

Changes in local government

After 1973, the newly set up Avon County Council took over responsibility for roads throughout a wider region. Its new Highways Dept had to hit the ground running and, staffed with many of the same councillors and officers as before, continued with the Outer Circuit Road policies of the previous local authority. (14) Avon inherited Totterdown's 'core site', now a wasteland, plus the majority of properties between Hill Avenue and the railway bridge on St

Luke's Road. It also inherited three of the 23 properties extending in the other direction between Hill Avenue and St John's Lane, which had been part of a longer-term road-widening scheme. The owner of number 63 St Luke's Road complained to the Council that he was both unable to sell his house but was also unable to get an improvement grant to enable him to stay in it, because the property was still under threat from the earlier road-widening scheme. Bristol City Council, which still managed properties within the city, requested Avon to remove the improvement line in a bid to remove this blight, but Avon refused. Number 63 is still there, in the surviving terrace, 45-65 St Luke's Road.

Bristol's local government re-organisation provided a lull which gave eviction respite for Totterdown although it was already too late; the middle of Totterdown was a desolate scene; the rest of Totterdown was depressed, there was nowhere left to shop or to meet whilst out shopping.

There was still one lonely house left in the new Totterdown prairie like a surviving tooth, 22 Highgrove Street - or rather three, because the two on each side were left to support it. Its owner, Mr Bradbeer, had stood out against the Council and refused to move. Avon's Planning & Transport Committee had negotiated a purchase price of £1,350 with him in 1972 and had offered Mr Bradbeer's tenant accommodation in Bedminster. Mr Bradbeer had then acquired a Council improvement grant (this possibly demonstrates a lack of inter-departmental communication), started work on his house and eventually tried to renegotiate the purchase price. The Council acknowledged that it was indeed worth more now, but there was no possibility of renegotiation. He was finally paid in 1975 and held out at his Highgrove Street fortress until then. (15) Because the *Evening Post* had championed him, he had become a city-wide symbol of Totterdown.

Henry Bradbeer holding a no doubt significant letter for the press. (BEP)

The recurring theme of 'The Last Three Houses in Totterdown'. The one in the middle is the legendary Henry Bradbeer's. The ones on each side are holding it up!

Blight in Totterdown

In 1975, Avon, who were worried by Totterdown's blighted state, started some reparation work and this took the form of a Housing Action Area in which specially run down property in a part of the Pylle Hill area could be rehabilitated. (16) The residents there were seen as secondary to the road scheme as 'the Action Area will inevitably be dominated by the requirements of the road network...the future use of the remainder of the land and the treatment of the surrounding built-up area.' Whilst this was happening, the Outer Circuit Road project continued and another two years of Totterdown's blight and depression ensued. Then in 1979 the highway scheme itself was axed, for financial reasons, but a reduced scheme dual carriageway and flyover plan for Totterdown's Three Lamps junction was substituted. (The reasons for both this and the eventual final cancellation of the highway scheme are discussed in Chap 5, p34) At that point the lost buildings tally was 550 gone plus eight houses on St Luke's Road, part-demolished. Solon Housing Association rehabilitated the latter for two-year emergency housing.

The new 'core site' (sic) prairie land in the middle of Totterdown provided yet more problems for locals. Clearance had taken place progressively as houses were acquired. The holes had been filled and levelled, the surface was re-soiled and seeded with grass and was maintained by the Estates Services Department using a tractor and hand mowers. Dangerous subsidence occurred occasionally over former cellars. These had to be re-excavated and backfilled for the second time. The whole area was: 'open to lorry parking, fly tipping, vehicle trespass, vandalism and household rubbish disposal' in Avon's own words.

Travellers at the bottom of Oxford Street. (BEP)

Travellers' camp handy for the Bath Road. (BEP)

Totterdown people were disgusted. (17) Avon discussed various ways to deal with these problems on what was its inherited land but decided not to fence it off as 'it would erode the public's freedom to walk on it'. In July 1981, travellers moved in. They were noted by the Council as 'visually obtrusive but not apparently causing a nuisance to locals'.(18) Reminiscences by local people suggest this was otherwise. The travellers called frequently on the neighbouring houses for water and other necessities of life as there were no facilities for them on the site. There were also stories of intimidation and petty theft which were not at this stage conveyed to the Council. (19)

The Committee, on the other hand, were apprehensive of the potential danger of more travellers arriving and their indecision about how to deal with the Totterdown travelers lead

The Bath Road end of the Totterdown prairie. (BEP)

them into beginning to devise a 'Gypsy Policy' which exercised them for several years. Meanwhile the Council's Solicitor was authorised to initiate court proceedings if numbers did increase. They could, thought the Committee, move them onto the official Patchway Gypsy Site and Avon would stand each of them the £50 admittance fee. However, they were reluctant to move them at that time as one of them was pregnant. The irony of this situation may have been felt by some councillors in view of the previous Council's policy to evict the legitimate occupiers of the site, regardless of their age, health or pregnancy status but if so, it goes unrecorded.

However, as if drawing the line under destruction and because there had been a call in Bristol to do so, Avon decided to replace the Three Lamps Signpost. In 1978 it discussed how best to renovate the sign and were preparing an estimate for its refurbishment and re-erection at what would be a site near to its original one as the configuration of the roads had changed. It had lain on its side in Dovercourt Road storage depot since 1972, latterly almost completely covered by brambles.

The careful refurbishment was carried out by the local Peter Wright Engineering firm and Peter Wright himself supervised the sign as it was craned and bolted into place, watched by many locals. During the following year the Civic Society and Totterdown people requested that the lighting, formerly gas, in the three globes on the sign be reinstated. Bristol Civic Society contributed 50 per cent of the required £1,000 but they were rebuffed by Avon (which had previously said the Society should pay the full amount), which returned it. Fortunately for all concerned, Peter Wright had had the forethought to install draw wires in the column so that electric cables could be used should the lights ever be needed in the future. (20) They were and the symbolic sign was restored to its rightful position much to the relief of the locals. This drew to an end the demolition and 12-year Blight period of Totterdown's history.

Evidently the BBC needed terrain like this for car stunts in its 1970s series 'Target'. Leading man, Patrick Mower filming in Totterdown in 1977. (BEP)

A summary

Totterdown survived what befell it, because it still contained the balance of a very close community which had been further cohered in mutual misery, lobbying and protest. This demolition was so long drawn out that times and ethos and public finance changed and Totterdown was rehabilitated and redeveloped in more of a spirit of conciliation than the Lawrence Hill area. The latter, typical of many similarly treated areas nationally, in 2000 had injected into it £50 million ten-year regeneration funding through the Government's New Deal scheme for management by local people to restore some of the facilities, safety and sense of community which had been destroyed in the 1960s.

4 Incredulity and Protest

The Planners did to us what the war could not do.
Elsie Lawrance, author of *Growing up in Totterdown 1922-1936*

Public incredulity over the 1966 local Road Plans had been widely expressed in Bristol – and Totterdown – and was pumped up through news coverage and letters in the Bristol press. The *Bristol Evening Post* highlighted much of the disbelief that people felt.

Before land acquisition in Totterdown had begun, the Totterdown Traders' Association had believed that the Council was 'unlikely to force Compulsory Purchase on 50 traders'. They saw themselves as a commercial body and less likely to be evicted than ordinary householders. Mr McCloud, newsagent formerly on Bath Road remembers: 'The shopkeepers went to see Gervas Walker because no-one from the Council came up to Totterdown'. Their assumption turned out to be wrong; Totterdown businesses were to be demolished too. In 1969 having consolidated their Association the Totterdown Traders drew up their own alternative road plan. When the Bristol Development Plan was published in 1966, Bristol artist Jerry Hicks ironically characterised it as part of a national conspiracy to heap on the city the worst of all planning in a bid to raise public consciousness and therefore save the rest of Britain from destruction. He called it the Dodo Project and lampooned it derisively. (1)

A decade on, Douglas Adams parodied a similar road development situation by having Arthur Dent lie in the path of a bulldozer which is fast approaching his front door to create a path for a by-pass because 'You've got to build by-passes'. Arthur has missed the significance of the plans which had been on display for nine months, but which he'd seen the afternoon before in the cellar of the Planning Office where the lights and stairs had gone, in the bottom of a locked filing cabinet stuck in a disused lavatory with a sign on the door saying Beware of the Leopard. This had militated against Arthur making his protest at the appropriate time. (2) This is a facetious reference but it echoes the surrealism of such situations.

There was an incredulity factor built into the interaction of the Bristol Council and its evictees, and also ordinary Bristol people and was the preliminary to an extreme test of people's tolerance thresholds. Evictees who moved out of the area and who have contributed their reminiscences are still incredulous that they and many others, who had no other option open and who believed they were making yet another national patriotic sacrifice, made it without the Outer Circuit Road ever actually having been built.

In their reminiscences, Totterdown evictees repeatedly expressed the amazement they felt about what was happening to them and that Council delegates had appeared, or affected not to understand their concerns. Councillors had underestimated these worries and acted as if they believed that Totterdown householders would and should welcome a move to the new and popular suburbs that others were flocking to by choice. Certainly this was the impression that evictees drew from talking to them. (3)

Totterdown was – and parts still are – densely populated and at least three to five family generations had lived and grown up in it. People were likely to be living in close proximity to other family members, within a very supportive environment. (4) Many houses in the 'Core' demolition site had been built with front doors opening straight onto the pavement. Although many had not been modernised by 1966 they were never slums and were in fact better-constructed houses than the earlier ones on Pylle Hill. (5)

To qualify as slums, terraced housing had to be 'back to back' with shared outside toilets and obviously unhealthy to live in. The 'core site' (6) Totterdown houses were not. Mike Leigh of Bristol Record Office had inside knowledge after house hunting there in the early '60s and describes them affectionately as 'little palaces'. Possibly the Council did really believe that they were giving the occupants an upgrading opportunity; that would certainly put a more altruistic spin on the matter. (7)

In 1971 an *Evening Post* letter read, somewhat patronisingly: 'It is quietly assumed in many places that the Outer Circuit Road may never be built through Clifton. Why should it degrade the quality of life for those living in lesser areas of the city?' Others could not believe that there would continue to be a demand for private cars and motorways: 'as car use would dwindle, petrol become short, cars smaller and city highways redundant'. (8)

At the rare Totterdown Public Information Meetings, Council personnel appeared to have so much faith in what they were doing, that they presented astonishment that Totterdowners were not reassured by their careful explanations to show why the planning decisions on roads and transport were exciting. They appeared incredulous that locals were not going to lie back and accept these changes. They had apparently assumed that residents would tolerate new busy highways traversing their locality providing they were offered tasteful landscaping and tree planting to screen them off.

This incredulity on both sides continued into the 1980s when Totterdown locals were not appeased by the opportunity to take part in decisions about crossings and bus lay-bys when they were actually concerned about and wanted shops to be replaced and the clearing up of the demolition site which they still had to live with. (9)

The Council's view of the 'Old and New' expressed in *Civic News* (10) about Kingsdown redevelopment was that (in the original Kingdown) 'All the picturesque was not grace and beauty...the streets were narrow, illuminated on dark evenings only by a few and far between oil lamps, whose feeble flickering lights often went out for lack of fuel'. When in 1958 the Council had decided to acquire all the Victorian terraced private properties there to roll out a regeneration scheme: 'Some had opposed public purchase because they wished to see preserved the character of that same Georgian development. A lament was raised for the passing of streets whose atmosphere reflected a quieter, less hurried world. Forgotten were the scenes of ribaldry and callousness that many of them had witnessed'.

This explanation was used to justify mass demolition in Kingsdown, parts of which almost immediately became a 'high ribaldry and callousness' crime spot and no-go area at night. Some incredulity was expressed by the Bristol Visual and Environmental Group that the only alternative to the dark satanic, poorly lit, areas without recreation space was complete demolition and the replacement by higher status houses for business people and tower blocks with open grassland surrounding them for the lower classes to live in and kick a ball about on. Although the 1960s are now symbolized by modernism, the Beatles and Carnaby Street, it was also the time of *Cathy Come Home*. It was the continued existence of British class system attitudes made the 'clean up' possible. (11)

In 1964 in East Bristol – 'Easton is regarded at the moment as an eyesore and a blot on the route from the city centre to suburbia' – was used to justify irreparable redevelopment in another close-knit community. 'New' had become a synonym for 'Better;' Anything old and labelled shabby was swept away. (12)

The beginnings of a new age of protest

In Bristol, incredulity soon turned to action and protest, mirroring what was taking place elsewhere in the country. Lobby groups were set up and existing ones re-energised. Many protesters networked with and were members of other groups lobbying against different development but with the same core concerns. This is probably the stage at which we can call Protest a movement rather than a series of localised single-issue campaigns. By 1968 there was a new age of protest nationally. Tony Benn, Labour MP for SE Bristol, including Totterdown, had been Minister of Technology in the Harold Wilson government since 1966, overseeing the 'White Heat of Technology' revolution (including the Concorde project in Bristol), that Harold Wilson saw as a primary tool to revive the British economy.

The background to protest was labour unrest and the 1968 students' uprising. Benn speaks of 'The troubled mood of the times...the pressure for the redistribution of political power will have to be faced...people want a much greater say'. One of the requirements he listed was: 'The Government's need to know more about the public's frame of mind'. In the first 6 months of 1968 more than three million working days had been lost to strikes. (13)

Between then and 1974, amenity societies, residents' groups, housing and action groups proliferated in Bristol in response to developments taking place affecting many neighbourhoods and linked by opposition to the Outer Circuit Road Plan. For once development impacted not only on workers' 'outdated' Victorian terraces but also threatened middle class localities with fine architecture, peopled by home owners with louder voices and a range of specialisms in housing, architecture, law, advice and conservation and the environment.

These people made sure their arguments were heard and acted as a catalyst, bringing groups along behind them. Environmentalism was on the rise in the 1960s and 1970s. In the background the Cold War rumbled on, which no-one could do anything about apart from demonstrating with CND; but more immediately tackle-able were the perceived results of Brave New Worldism in Science, Technology and Industry all of which seemed doomed to result in eco as well as health damage (14) not to mention destructive changes to the city environment in people's own back yards.

Environmental activists had the knowledge to argue with policy and attack issues, citing financial profligacy, unnecessary destruction and the possibility that alternative, more sensible options were also open. In Bristol these campaigns mushroomed to address threats to the former City Docks and Suspension Bridge locality by publicly countering development plans with ingenious and workable policies provided by the professionals within the general public.

These Bristol-wide spokespeople represented the very public opinions and counter-plans that Councillors Jenkins and Walker were sceptical of and saw as a bar to progress – particularly the Clifton lobby, which they both hated. (15) The new campaign lobbyists were perhaps more city-interested over self-interested than Jenkins and Walker believed with regard to the Council's plans to cover the old Floating Harbour over to create a new, valuably-located real estate area. A private proposal to build skyscraper flats for the rich with the Clifton Suspension Bridge for their backdrop was also in the pipeline in the late 1970s.

The leader of the Avon Gorge Campaign was Paul Chadd, a barrister-activist, working out of the Guildhall Chambers, Broad Street. Craig Begg, a Solicitor working *pro bono* for the Civic Society, was also prominent in this group. In the early 1970s he also formed the Bristol Planning Group composed of academics which opposed the 1967 City Docks closure plan. Both groups contained members common to both and networked with each other. (16)

Another Clifton-based activist was John Grimshaw, a civil engineer, involved in the City Docks protest around 1970 and 1971. (17) These people were a new and unexpected challenge to Planning Leaders as they could not be dismissed in the stereotypical way as Trades Union stirrers, loony lefties, or uninformed woolly-hatted idealists; they were part of Bristol's influential professional classes.

The central focus of many of the campaigns of the time was to point out that there was never any examination of more than the one option for development on the table. The Council's position was that the status quo got in the way of modernism and 'clean-sweepism' which favoured the destruction of past architecture or infrastructure as the only way forward. The campaigners advocated searching for sound proposals which were less socially damaging and did not favour the car over and above people. In connection with road building, John Grimshaw recently said that as a civil engineer he had felt it was part of his brief to examine a client's request for a road design and use his expertise to advise whether a new road was actually what was needed and that there weren't other creative solutions to the problem. (18)

Another key person to the Protest Movement was David Hirschmann, living in Redland and a Philosophy lecturer at Bristol University from 1960. In 1968 Hirschmann's wife had started Shelter in Bristol, (Shelter had been set up in 1966, shortly after Cathy Come Home aired) and he had helped to run the St Paul's Advisory Service. By 1970 with the news that central Government had approved the Bristol Outer Circuit Road plan, in principle if not in detail, Hirschmann set up and co-ordinated an anti-Road campaign. News was spreading that properties were being acquired in Easton and Totterdown. People in those affected areas woke up at last, local groups came together to oppose the road and went into direct action. (19)

At this stage, for the Outer Circuit Road protest at least, support from the local press was vital. The *Evening Post*, under its Editor, community-minded Gordon Farnsworth and with Totterdown resident Gerry Brooke as Chief Librarian, strongly supported the anti-Road lobby and any piece of news about Totterdown or the Road was seized upon. (20) (Gerry later set up the Totterdown Action Group with his next door neighbour, Bob Taylor).

The Montpelier Residents' Association (anti-Road) was launched in the *Evening Post* and was soon joined by the launch of the St Paul's Action Group – an offshoot of the Housing Group, spearheaded by David Hirschmann. Hirschmann persuaded the different groups which were forming along the Outer Circuit Road line to unite for better effect. It was decided they would function under an umbrella committee chaired by Hirschmann but would also remain autonomous. This was a good move because the groups from more advantaged areas of the city could not be characterised by politicians as middle class gentrifiers and conservationists and those from less advantaged areas as: 'Owners of shabby 100 year old terraced houses due for demolition anyway'. Initially the anti-Road lobby needed to

The Three Lamps pub was *not* demolished. It was empty and squatted in 1988. (BEP)

convince local councillors that building the Road was a foolish plan which they would come to regret. (21) In 1967 the Bristol Civic Society and Bristol Society of Architects advanced detailed objections to the Plan based on cost and destruction levels. (22) No record has been found by this writer that the protest groups ever campaigned to have the whole scheme stopped; instead they campaigned to rationalize it and re-route it so that it was not so environmentally and socially damaging.

At this time the correspondence sections of the local press, particularly the *Evening Post*, was gridlocked with letters on the Outer Circuit Road – mainly anti – and it has to be said that there was a minority in favour of it. There was also much derisory comment published elsewhere. Architect George Ferguson, then newly arrived in Bristol and now President of ARIBA, described his early days in the city: 'I did not know how the planning of Bristol was in the grip of highway engineers with more regard for Los Angeles-style spaghetti junctions and urban motorways than for the traditions and people of such a rich and varied city'. George described Walker and Jenkins as: 'powerful but misguided politicians and their apparent resolve to destroy the best of Bristol, was eventually to drive me briefly into the Planning Department and into the local politics of the 70s'. (23)

In 1967 the Totterdown Traders' Association which had formed because they soon realised they were not at all a special case, drew up their own plan and this was the beginning of alternative Road layout plans suggested by Totterdown. (24)

In 1971 the Bristol and Environmental Group was set up by Dorothy Brown 'To fight for

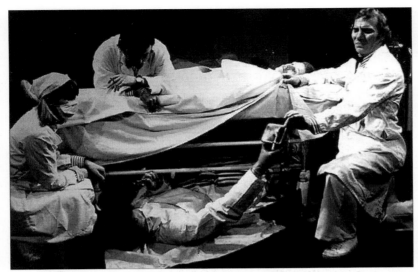

A scene from 'Bristol Road Show', with Pete Postlethwaite and the Company treating a patient mentally disturbed enough to WALK to work. (Images by Derek Balmer in the Bristol University Theatre Collection)

the character of Bristol' and it produced pictorial publications demonstrating the disastrous course of planning in the City and the destruction going on.

By 1971, Hirschmann's St Paul's Action Group and the Montpelier Residents' Association had galvanised their fight along the line of the affected Outer Circuit Road areas to demonstrate for change. By the Autumn of 1971 the Campaign against the Road began to establish itself, with three delegates preparing a sound case for an alternative route. The Campaign was not formally constituted but continued so successfully as a strong umbrella support for anyone against the Road that by 1972 the public believed it was an official organization. This was caused by the spin given to it by the *Evening Post* which was then picked up by the *Times*. It encouraged protesters to write to Peter Walker, the Secretary of State and in November 1971 it had enlisted Bristol University students to leaflet the threatened areas so that residents had more information and could voice better-informed objections.

This new campaign was launched, supported by the *Evening Post* and continued solidly for six months. The leafleting was concentrated on Easton where the Road plan was furthest advanced, then Cotham, Clifton, Totterdown and Southville. (25) Gervas Walker, then Chair of Planning, and his Labour Shadow Wally Jenkins, with absolutely no sense of irony, accused the students and their lecturers of conducting a 'Consternation campaign that would frighten little old ladies to death and which was disturbing the community'. (26)

At that time both political parties within the Council were enthusiastically in support of the Road scheme, seeing it as the path to prosperity. In the same year, Paul Chadd, who had become known as 'Champion of the Environmentalists' demanded of the Planning Dept:

'Scrap this savage plan…roads must not become the sex symbols of planners', and he promoted an alternative plan.

The protest was then ratcheted up a slot with a public meeting in St Paul's, officiated over by campaign leader David Hirschmann and the city barrister Paul Chadd, by urging a full scale campaign against the Road Plan. (27) Meetings of St Paul's and Montpelier Action Groups were reported every day in the *Evening Post*.

In a *Post* interview the City Engineer admitted that the effect on Montpelier was a strong feature of the criticism of the Outer Circuit Road. He promised that 'it would not be constructed there within 15 years'. (28) Then came the merest small shifting of opinion as early the next year, Bristol's Borough Labour Council made a policy statement with a request that any further work on the Road Plan be delayed at least until the LUTS (Land Use and Transportation Study) report, now commissioned by the Council, was complete two years further down the line. Arthur Palmer, Labour Member of Parliament for Bristol Central tabled a Commons question over the examination of Bristol's major roads. Later he continued to campaign against the Road as he also pointed out, little had been said about the upcoming LUTS study. (29)

1972 was to be a year of action and flurries of Council activity in Bristol and in Totterdown. Other campaign groups – the Bristol Council of Christian Churches and Joint Action Bedminster arose and the first press mention of Totterdown and Lower Knowle Community Association appears. The Hirschmann Umbrella Group arranged for Bedminster and Totterdown to be leafleted to explain how the Road plan would affect them, including the fact that Victoria Park would be split in two.

After years of prevarication and apparently now beginning to feel the pressure, Wally Jenkins promised a decision on the Road Plan within two months. He did not deliver on this. In Bristol, relentless lobbying of local and national politicians continued throughout the year and a protest stage show called The Bristol Road Show was mounted at the freshly established Bristol New Vic. The Show's author was David Illingworth (who wrote for Avon Touring) and the company had some notable members including Director Howard Davies, nowadays Associate Director if the National Theatre and starting-out actor Pete Postlethwaite. The play included satirical songs and informed, ironic and incisive script. Bristol politicians Graham and Valerie Davey who saw the show, remember that the second half opened with the actors asking members of the audience to move to different seats: 'all those asked on the night we were there complied obediently just as the residents of Totterdown mostly accepted their re-location'.

The play was written to challenge. Belly Acher (a protester) engaged in sword and dialogue thrusts in which he charged Towny Planner with constructing the first section of Outer Circuit Road before statutory permission had been given or any enquiry held and that he had proposed the Outer Circuit Road before making traffic assessments. Belly Acher satirized the lofty and shortsighted aspirations of the Planners to the extent that Tony Benn, MP for East Bristol and Totterdown, publicly recommended Bristol Road Show to Council members. The reaction of the angry audience was to shout out for Councillors to 'show themselves'. (30) There was public discussion following the performance and on one night, the Road Show's cast joined in a combined Friends of the Earth and Road Protest Groups' vigil on College Green. (31)

The uncertainty and Protest pressure was also beginning to affect the Councillors representing the inner suburbs. There was added uncertainty for Councillors who now knew that a radical local government re-organisation was coming and a new, geographically larger County of Avon Council would supersede the present City Council. (32) Windmill Hill Ward Labour Councillor Richards, mindful of this, told people that the fact that the Outer Circuit Road was grant-aided, (ie it was part-funded by central Government), had a big bearing on whether it would: 'come here or not...there may be a reassessment of the situation'. Meanwhile houses that had been compulsorily purchased still had to be demolished because vagrants and looters targeted them. (33) In June 1972 the Civic Society called on the Government's Environment Secretary, Geoffrey Rippon for a review and to call-in Stages 2 and 3 of the Road. The following month, a 900-signature petition from Ashton, Bedminster and Southville, asking for a halt on the Outer Circuit Road until after the LUTS study was published was received by the Council. (34)

5 Protest – the personnel and the politicisation

The City Council had just lost its attempt to fill in the city docks, thereby creating a good bit of real estate, but had been defeated by the citizens.
John Grimshaw, recalling the protest movement

In 1972, Bristol Council had been pressing the Department of the Environment for a clear statement on the future of the Road Plan and Alderman Jenkins had now become rehabilitated as a hero for doing the pressing. (1) By the autumn, with Labour in power, the LUTS report a year in preparation so far but not yet published, there was a degree of back-pedalling going on whilst the Council – about to be superseded by a new highways authority – awaited its recommendations. The Labour party hedged its bets by talking about a modified Road route and by pledging that the Road Plan would not continue past Totterdown. (2)

By August 1972 with work on stages 2 and 3 of the Road still scheduled to start the following year, there was no commitment for it to go further, though this would be defined by the LUTS survey. With more back pedalling, a new modified scheme was under discussion which would reduce the number of lanes down to two instead of three in each direction. Alderman Wally Jenkins, now Chair of the Planning Department, (with Gervas Walker his Shadow Chair), was heard to say that it was a 'very acceptable solution to short term traffic difficulties'. A start could be made on tidying up Totterdown and shortly afterwards the 'tidying up Totterdown' plan was explained by the Council to Totterdown at a local public meeting. It involved landscaping with trees, walls and safety fencing, all of which was publicly derided by Bristol Civic Society. (3)

The meeting was also attended by John Grimshaw, prominent in the City Docks campaign and at that time working as a Civil Engineer for and representing Manders & Partners; TKAG (Totterdown and Knowle Action Group) had asked Manders to draw up an alternative plan for the Totterdown stretch – the whole Road route between St Philip's Marsh and Bedminster. (4) Totterdown's action groups slip in and out of news events. In 1972 the Totterdown Traders' Assocation, chaired by Lloyd Keen, comes into view and also in this year the Totterdown and Lower Knowle Tenants' Association was formed by Councillor Chris Reid. Reid had by then lived for 30 years in Totterdown and claimed the Association was the 'Voice of Totterdown'. Despite his opposition to the Road in the Totterdown community in which he lived, Chris Reid was a member of the Council which was driving ahead the Road Plans and he is not recorded as having demurred in meetings about them. Later on in November 1977 Councillor Reid would pursue his locally supportive position as Chair of

END OF AN ERA:
THE BATH AND WELLS SIGN BEING
REMOVED   5TH MARCH 1973

Photos above and on page 55; these were used for a TAG protest. (BEP)

TAG in Bush Telegraph as: 'hoping for some change now that TAG had been set up with the objective of achieving a better Totterdown'. (5)

It is not clear now what the connection between these various Totterdown groups was and how much they overlapped. During 1972 the Totterdown and Knowle Action Group had formed to fight the Road plans and had met several times. (6) In 1972 the Totterdown Traders' Assocation, chaired by Lloyd Keen, appears and also that year the Totterdown and Lower Knowle Tenants' Association was formed by Councillor Chris Reid. At an unknown date TCA (Totterdown Community Association) came into being and was the forerunner of TACA (Totterdown Area Community Association) which was to be constituted in 1986 for the purpose of negotiating Zone A from the Council, (described in Chapter 8).

Meanwhile TAG, (Totterdown Action Group), was formed around 1977/8 by Gerry Brooke and Bob Taylor, Totterdown neighbours, after the demolition. Members met regularly at the Housing Advice Centre to arrange protests and events. Gerry Brooke made sure Totterdown was kept in the public eye in terms of news coverage and in pictures. Consequently the *Post* still has a rich archive of Totterdown photos, many of which are reproduced in this book. Radio Bristol got involved during Totterdown's Housing Action period in the Pylle Hill area, making regular visits to Henry Street to follow the lives of its residents. This appears to have been for the collection of local history, but it all kept Totterdown on the map. (7) A group letter from 45 residents in Totterdown's Stevens Crescent, was published in the *Evening Post* describing how the new road would split the community. (8)

John Grimshaw, nowadays Chief Executive of SUSTRANS, arrived in Bristol in 1970 and describes his involvement in the wider Bristol Protest Movement and the anti-Road Plan in

Totterdown. 'I was appalled to find that no provision had been made in Bristol for cycling so I immediately got going on that. On my own doorstep, the City Council had just lost its attempt to fill in the city docks, thereby creating a good bit of real estate, but had been defeated by the citizens. We set up the City Docks Group to bring new ideas to that decaying area; we didn't do a huge amount but we did set up the ferry company and bought back the cranes which had been sold – just before the scrap merchant took them down. Paul Chadd was involved with the protest against the filling-in of the Docks and Craig Begg (a solicitor) agreed to provide professional services. Paul held Breakfast Meetings and briefed everyone on what they had to do before going into enquiries. This raised the game'. Explaining how different this new age of protest was John Grimshaw said: 'Paul Chadd was the sort of person usually on the side of the developers, but he became involved in the Avon Gorge protest; he was the QC who was retained by the Civic Society to fight off the tower block that was planned for the site. We did lose in respect of the demolition of Totterdown. Then LUTS happened which stalled everything and was the start of another series of studies. The failure to get the light metro was the first of a long series of failures. You have to be very cynical about these studies which are not done to bring change but to cement an existing point of view. (9)

Attempts to make things better in Totterdown

This reminiscence from John Grimshaw shows how the protest movement in Bristol mirrored the national one through being peopled by members with professional expertise who networked across and linked together the various protests and attempts to bring in new ideas. At the same time, John Grimshaw and Sue Learner took other direct action in Totterdown to counter the blight and depression in the area. (10)

In November there was another two-hour crowded Totterdown Public Meeting set up by the Council and chaired by Windmill Hill Labour Cllr Graham Robertson. Vice Chair of the Planning Committee Brian Richards stood in for the absent Chair, Alderman Wally Jenkins. Tony Benn, the local MP was in the audience as were some unnamed councillors. The meeting was to outline plans for landscaping options, clearing up Totterdown and new shops.

Local people became explosively angry; they warmly applauded a resident who declared they: 'did not want a fairy park – we want houses or shops built on that dump and peace and quiet for me and my neighbours'. The Secretary of the Totterdown and Knowle Community Association was told that the alternative road scheme TKCA had commissioned from Manders and Partners was not feasible from an engineering standpoint although Manders had assured Richards this was not so. Gradients used were in excess of what the Ministry would allow and there were other discrepancies. When a man in the balcony shouted out 'This is disgusting!' Robertson closed the meeting. (11)

Graham Davey, then the local Green Party candidate, remembers chairing a similarly explosive meeting at some date in Totterdown at the Methodist Church Hall during which part of the ceiling fell down. Tony Benn who was speaking, seized on this as a demonstration of the need to regenerate the area rather than to build the Road. There were no local Councillors present and a small group left the meeting to carry its message of opposition to the Road to Councillor Sprackling. He was absent due to a social function to mark the end of the term of service of the Lord Mayor and he subsequently wrote to the *Evening Post* complaining about a posse being sent to get him. (12)

By December 1972 the protest movement had become politicised within the official Labour Party. The 'Stop the Road' Labour Committee of 1973 was set up 'to personally co-ordinate all activities directed towards the Outer Circuit Road in Bristol as well as looking into roads policy'. David Hirschmann was on this Committee together with three councillors from Bristol and Somerset wards. Hirschmann was accused of having set up his campaign as a front for the Labour Party. (13) This was a period of great uncertainty punctuated with leaks of information, vacillation, intrigues and splits within the parties. Conscious of this, the Montpelier and St Paul's Groups kept up the pressure, widening the brief and opposing the most recent plans to bring the M32 link road through their area. (14) In June 1973, the residents' groups canvassed the Totterdown area and produced a petition demanding the Council remove the prevailing Blight. They also campaigned to improve public transport. The South Bristol Railway had survived the 1960s Beeching cuts but services were reduced. They called for the improvement of services, an improved timetable and a more efficient bus service. (15) On 22 June 1973 the Government Transport Minister John Peyton, also Tory MP for Yeovil, backed the modified Road Programme Stages 2 and 3. This flurry preceded the long awaited Interim LUTS Report which was due to be published in 10 days.

Other people in Totterdown attempted to keep community spirit going amidst the gloom. In 1973 the affectionately remembered Totterdown Festival was inaugurated for this purpose. (16) In December the Methodist Church had held its Anniversary celebrations and evidently Totterdown had felt that one of their tormenters had now been sufficiently neutralised by being made Mayor of Bristol for there is a record of the Lord Mayor and Lady Mayoress Alderman and Mrs Wally Jenkins joining in the Methodist Morning Service on 25 November 1973. (17)

Then after 1 April 74 there came a gap during which the Council re-adjusted itself following local government re-organisation and the new County of Avon was created. Avon was

HOW MUCH 'PUBLIC OPEN SPACE' IS ACTUALLY NEEDED ? OR WILL WE GET IT ANYWAY BECAUSE OF THE CUTS ? HOW CAN WE MAKE IT USEABLE ? Graveyard for Avon CC.

Another TAGs protest exhibition photo asking pertinent questions – someone has added their own interpretation of the space: 'Graveyard for Avon CC'.

now responsible for Highways, Transport and Strategic Planning over the increased county area which included parts of Somerset and Gloucestershire; the Bristol Council continued with local planning and development taking place within the former city area. In the early days this was a recipe for confusion and some Council in-fighting. (18) In the short term it made no change to the Totterdown part of the road plan with the long overdue LUTS report rumoured to be concerned more with the post-Totterdown stage of the Road. Even if it had been, it was already too late for the over 550 shops and houses which had already been demolished in Totterdown, even before Phases 2 and 3 of the Outer Circuit Road had been approved in detail. (19)

Other influences began to be felt; the commercial property market collapsed following boom years in the late 1960s and early 1970s and £25 million was cut from major road expenditure. (20) At the same time, public opinion was running against relentless destruction and feelings in Bristol ran high against the Bristol Development Plan roads. (21) David Starkie points out that there were probably also protests within Government and cites Richard Crossman and Tony Benn as likely suspects. Tony Benn does not confirm or refute that, but has shown in various publications that he was not sympathetic to the rush towards car transport and highway building. (22)

However, the Council's faith was still pinned on Clean Sweepism and in a failed Public

Relations exercise to lift the Blight which by then had settled on Montpelier, it demolished a terrace of Victorian houses there and rebuilt expensively on its site. (23) The Council later redeemed itself with an apology. (The development was demolished in 2000.) Instead, the Council turned to refurbishing existing houses, taking advantage of Government legislation to give special treatment to depressed areas – and this is what Totterdown would presently benefit from. (24) However, in November 1975, Totterdown child Adrian Williams aged eight, had written in Bush Telegraph about his imagined world in 2075: 'I see a world of spaghetti junctions'.

In fact, 1975 brought more financial disasters as the national property market collapsed altogether and local government spending was cut. Accordingly both Avon and Bristol produced policies restricting commercial development and road building. In the same year the LUTS Report was published at last. In respect of the Outer Circuit Road component, LUTS cited adverse environmental effect, low economic benefit, and probable non-effectiveness and therefore recommended that it should cut off at, and not be built beyond, Totterdown.

In 1975, Bristol designated Housing Action Areas in St Paul's then in 1977 extended it to Lower Montpelier, to carry out the same kind of work under way in Totterdown. But Totterdown had already been reduced to a blighted wasteland and irrevocable damage had been done to Easton's community by intermixed clean sweepism, rehousing policy and Road building. This blight would linger for decades. There was a wind of change blowing, though, and in 1977, the Conservation Advisory Panel was set up. (25)

But that wind hadn't arrived in Totterdown yet. In 1979 Cllr Mather Bell and his Avon Officers told members of TAG: 'There can be no further public meetings and that the plans (for a reduced Road Scheme) will go ahead over the next eighteen months. Cllr Chris Read opined: 'This, of course is quite unacceptable to Totterdown people, many of whom expressed their views at the last public meeting and I think the time has come to seek help from the Minister of Environment.'

In 1979, the Council agreed to the LUTS recommendations. That action and the Conservative cuts programme finally killed off the Outer Circuit Road plan itself. (26) However this was not the end of the matter for Totterdown because this decision was followed by a new series of Council plans for road improvements at Three Lamps junction. Arthur Howell wrote with weary hindsight in Bush Telegraph: 'Soon publicity caravans will be parked in the area with more detailed maps and information... the public meeting takes place in January and this must find us ready to talk to the Planners face to face'. Howell declared himself ready to set the ball rolling to come up with a viable alternative and he offered a £5 prize for young people to participate. It was the young people's future the

Planners were deciding and they would have to come up with a suggestion. (It is not recorded whether anyone did.) (27)

Angry Totterdown residents were now calling for the heart to be put back in Totterdown, shopping facilities to be provided again and play space provided for local children but to their incredulity, other road improvements were apparently still in the pipeline for Totterdown. An only marginally less environmentally damaging plan for a modernistic flyover had been substituted for the former 4-level transport interchange centre plan. It was explained to them during the next public meeting in Totterdown, chaired by Dawn Primarolo, that the Planners had decided that in order to include children's play areas in this next scheme, as Totterdown had requested, more houses would have to be demolished to make room. (28)

A model of this new scheme was on display in 1980 in the window of Avon House and an *Evening Post* letterwriter had dubbed it 'the Substitute Chiswick Flyover'. This name

Graham Cole of TAG masquerading at the Rump Scheme protest with a horse loaned for the occasion from SORCY. (BEP)

caught on and became its Bristol nickname. (29) In March TAG arranged an Action Day in Totterdown against the flyover – which TAG called 'The Rump Scheme'. There was a fancy dress march to the middle of Totterdown for a mass signing of a petition against the road scheme, followed by street theatre and music.

There was a rare piece of protest which happened during a Council meeting in March 1980. Councillor White materialised during an Avon debate on 'The Totterdown Situation' and accused the Council of having been unduly influenced by the eligibility of the scheme for a 75 per cent grant if the contract had been agreed by April 1982. He then pointed to the difference in the land cost for the Committee's scheme when it had been considered by the Resources Co-ordination Committee. White appears to be the first and only Councillor who spoke out against Totterdown's Road Scheme of that time. He stated his belief that it was unnecessary and that he would be able to convince the Committee that there were viable less costly alternatives that would enable more land to be released for redevelopment. He asked that the Committee consider the effect it would have on the local community.

However, The Committee Chair supported the County Engineer who still believed that their Department's scheme would be the best answer to the traffic problem and would release the maximum amount of land. His concern was to make an early decision 'in order all could see redevelopment take place'. The County Engineer was to prepare a report for the next meeting at which time the Committee resolved to approve and adopt it. (30)

TAG's 600-signature petition, (the Rump petition above), had been noted by Avon and a Motion was agreed that: 'There is sufficient public concern shown by the residents and groups within the Totterdown and Lower Knowle areas to justify a postponement of the plan to build the (lesser) Three Lamps Totterdown Road Improvement Scheme as previously agreed by the Council. This Council agrees to review the plans in six month's time to allow all the residents and interested parties the opportunities of jointly, with representatives of Avon County Council, fully debating the alternatives to the scheme'. Councillor White then pointed out that the scheme had been explained already at several public meetings with the outcome that: 'There is a feeling of frustration among local residents at the apparent unwillingness of the County Council to appreciate their opposition and to consider the alternatives available'. Apparently Council representatives had been transparent in not considering possible alternatives at a recent meeting with TAG which had included amended highway layouts and traffic management measures.

Avon's hand was forced by finance and later in the same year – 1980 – came the news that it had scrapped the 'Chiswick Flyover' plan 'for financial reasons' and had accepted 'a lesser scheme'. (31) In a wave of press publicity, TAG's Chair, Florence Portch, was triumphant. It was at this time during a public meeting in Totterdown, Cllr Chris Reid called for the Three Lamps signpost to be brought back.

6 The End of the Road Scheme – Retrospection Time

They uprooted people who had been there all their lives. Totterdown was ripped apart...
all for nothing.
Brenda Spriggs formerly resident on Summer Hill

It is likely that this overall protest from such a disparate front had affected the local Council. It had certainly affected its composition by the late 1970s, as protesters had networked with and infiltrated the Labour Group within it. However, it took a combination of factors – local government re-organisation, budget-stretching, political realignments and shifts and the end of the boom years and entry into the bust years, to kill off the Road plans. Once again, this was an echo of the national picture.

In 1981, George Micklewright, Bristol City Councillor for 23 years up to 2002 wrote a retrospective paper: 'How it Happened in Totterdown', analysing who the 'they' were who had carried out the Totterdown destruction. Micklewright admits to having lived in Totterdown in 1966 but claimed no recollection of the decision to build the Outer Circuit Road and therefore to demolish. (This is another indicator that no discernable advance warning had been made to Totterdown of how it featured in the Plan.) He wrote that the decision was never voted on in the Council as such but 'was a consequence of the decision to adopt the 1966 Development Plan in which it was incorporated'.

The City Council Minutes, he said, record no opposition to this report on either of the two occasions a vote was taken on it. The Tory Group supported the decision but the Council had a substantial Labour majority at the time. The Chair of the Planning Committee was Walter (Wally) Jenkins who in 1981 at the time of the paper was the Chair of the Docks Committee. Amongst the other suspects were a number of both Tories and Labourites and the (1981) Chair of the Planning Committee, Brian Richards.

Micklewright points out that Richards was a Councillor for Windmill Hill Ward (in which Totterdown lies) at the time and therefore an accomplice, without evidence to the contrary, (found neither by Micklewright or this writer) to the decision to decimate 'his own'. Fourteen members of the 1966 Labour Group – (Labour had a substantial majority over the Tories on the Council at the time) – were still members of the 1981 Labour Group and the rebuilding of Totterdown was in their hands. He points this out because when the 'final' Road Plan was cancelled, the press was full of letters and articles from Labour councillors claiming political victory through their lobbying.

The Group was: Wally Jenkins, Vic Pople, Brian Richards, Charles Merrett, Jack Fisk, Bert

Wilcox, Daisy Jackson, Jack Wood, Bert Abrams, Graham Robertson, Jeanette Britton, Iris Knight, Len Smith and George Maggs. Richards was one of three Labour candidates who lost their seats when (predictably) Windmill Hill went Tory three times in succession.

In 1973 Jenkins had been 'got rid of' by the conventional method of making him Lord Mayor, continues Micklewright's paper, (and this is the guise in which he turned up in Totterdown for the Methodist Church celebrations.) (1) Ironically the three men who had not apparently raised any protest before and who were still members of the Planning Committee were being entrusted to plan the rebuilding of Totterdown whose destruction they had agreed to. 'There is irony in that if nothing else', ends Micklewright. (2) This critique was significantly affected by internal Labour Party politics. The other irony is that Micklewrightism, which shaped the City Council's strategic approach for the best part of 20 years, was not very different from the patrician approach which saw a chunk of Totterdown flattened because the Council 'knew best'.

The incredulity – and now disgust – of Totterdown evacuees now centres on the fact that the road and interchange were never built. There is a suggestion that their loss might have been borne if it had been. Paul Attwell is still 'flaming mad'. Brenda Spriggs did not know many people who had been evicted and though she was not one of them, she says: 'We were devastated. They uprooted people who had been there all their lives...all for nothing.' An excerpt from a meeting reported in *Bush Telegraph* records resident Mrs R Blake saying of a speaker: 'She put everyone's feelings into words with her closing remark: We shouldn't mind so much if they had made the road, but to leave us like this...'

Totterdown is over-run by traffic around its perimeters and its residential roads are clogged with cars. Local people put up with it in order to live in Totterdown. Although the traffic situation is far from ideal, by using the 'Lesser Scheme' – much gentler road-widening, traffic diverting and traffic calming methods of the Council's Totterdown Action Plan, (described in the next chapter), the traffic has kept moving and a terminal gridlock situation as feared in the 1960 and '70s has not so far ever been reached.

This may be altered if Bristol City Council, South West Regional Development Agency and Bristol waterside Arena Ltd push ahead on their planned new 10,000-seater entertainment arena sited immediately north of Totterdown, beginning 2008. Two plus years in, there has been no consultation in Totterdown.

'On tick' in Totterdown – the Council and money

Back at the beginning of the story again in 1968, the Government was promising small loans of £2,500 to assist in the acquisition of land and the Ministry of Housing held its first

Enquiry with the results to be published in 1970. In Totterdown, houses were already boarded up and 'For Sale' signs, unsellable houses and derelict sites proliferated. David Hirschmannn and the various groups were just getting the Protest going.

When in 1970 the Council's Planning Committee met to consider the plan, the Outer Circuit Road from Lawrence Hill to Three Lamps was to cost £10m – but predictably that cost spiralled. The Plan has staged building and demolition built into it. Both political factions on the Council were in favour of the Road Plan, with no modifications. (3)

By 1972, the Council's plans for the Road's Stage 1 (Lawrence Hill) had begun with a projected completion date in 1973. The City Treasurer reported to the Council that the Road would only be regarded as Key Sector Expenditure IF it was approved by the Secretary of State for the Environment; but if it were to be referred to the City Council instead, its costs would probably have to be met by the 'Locally Determined Allocation.' However, to free up the land, all demolition had to be carried out in the first six months of the Contractor's contract.

So it appears that when it began, the clearance work for the road had not yet been approved at Government level and the source of funding for it had not yet been determined. In other words, the demolition was being carried out by the contractor and those houses would be lost whether the Road had been approved or not. Later that year the Lawrence Hill to Totterdown stretch was approved by Government but at that stage there was no commitment to build it beyond Totterdown. In December 1972 Mrs Cotton in St John's Lane asked in the *Evening Post*: 'Why must demolition start on any area before the Planners have made a definite decision on those plans? Homes have been pulled down, shops and premises boarded up and then we are told that the Planners do not need the ground after all.'

Government loans could not be sanctioned until the scheme was in the Minister's firm programme, but it evidently wouldn't be in the firm programme if the basis for it hadn't been laid, so Bristol Council had to authorise the City Valuer to proceed urgently with his acquisition negotiations. Obviously the acquisition was to acquire the land but the houses had to be demolished to free it up. Properties up to the £2,500 mark could be purchased in anticipation of those Government loans and the City Engineer and Treasurer decided to make temporary 'Land Acquisition' funds available pending sanctions on those loans.

None of the scheme came cheap. The cost of purchasing the smaller Totterdown houses (£1,000-£2,000) and their demolition (costing £90), were the lowest individual costs until multiplied over an area where 550 houses stood. Added to that there was Disturbance to Business compensation, which a few people managed to negotiate. Then there was the Search for, and Settlement with, the landowner and the Council's legal work throughout.

The most serious expense incurred was the planning and research carried out by the

New Statesman, September 1972.

external Civil Engineers. The state of the ground designated to support a four-level interchange was critical. Four tenders to carry out the soil survey at Totterdown had been made and Freeman Fox and Co were chosen to build the interchange. Freeman Fox had been involved in many major schemes around Bristol from the 1966 Severn Bridge and the Cumberland Basin Flyover. For the Outer Circuit Road 'spec', Freemans carried out all the design of the structures and road alignment and if the job had carried on, they would have done all the detailed structures design. When it was cancelled, Freeman Fox were authors of the design for the 'Chiswick Flyover' scheme which superceded it. When those plans were dropped, Freeman Fox designed the new road layout around Three Lamps Junction. This gives a sketch of the magnitude of the scheme and how much work had been carried out – and paid for – before the plan was aborted. Freeman Fox's fees including the soil surveys, the suspension testing (not explained) plan component came to £750,000. This was in turn a component of their total costs for Stages 2 and 3 (which were aborted) stated in their original plan to be £10,560,000. Their pedestrian and cycleway access to the Three Lamps Interchange Centre was a £100,000 part of this total. (4) In *Bristol Illustrated* magazine, April 1972, the total cost of Stages 2 ands 3 were quoted by 'A Citizen' as being in the region of £13m. This included the land purchase which the maths show must have been £2.5. *But it is hoped* continues 'A Citizen' *that a grant from the Department of the Environment would be received for 75% of the cost* but that depended on the Council acquiring the properties for the Council to meet its deadline by the middle of the year – June 1972. So despite the Skeffington Report of 1968 recommending a 9-point plan for Public Participation in Planning, it was central government's grant carrot with a deadline on it which drove local authorities onward in demolition. This sounds to a non-expert like implicit sanction. In the Bristol Road Show, Belly Acher points out that in 1967 at the Enquiry into the Outer Circuit Road, protesters were given 3 months to prepare their case. Under the 1971 Plan, they had been given only 6 weeks. Possibly the above deadline was the reason.

It also shows yet again that planning and managing the scheme was a surreal budget-

The tip of the triangle on the former Three Lamps junction is being cut right back to make way for the new slip road. (BEP)

juggling act involving timescales, projected 'approvals' and interim loans. Only the surviving council personnel know whether their belief in this huge scheme overrode anxiety keeping them awake at night.

Money again – boom to bust

When 1978 arrived, Avon had been anxious to crack on with the 'Chiswick Flyover' plan, substituted for financial reasons. It needed to get more Compulsory Purchase Orders approved to make way for the Flyover in Totterdown, including re-siting the Esso Garage which was negotiating with them more robustly than the residents had. By 1980 it became obvious that this hurry was because the cost of the land acquired before April 1975 would be eligible for a specific grant if the scheme was contracted to go before April 1982. (5)

By 1980, with the 'Chiswick Flyover' Plan also cancelled, another revised and reduced outlay (£4.75m down to £1.95m) plan for Three Lamps Junction was on the drawing board because costs had again to be reduced. Remembering that the objective of any plan was to relieve the Three Lamps Junction bottleneck, a fresh measure suggested was to build a new Angers Road to connect the Bath and Wells Road, but there was no immediate guaranteed finance even for this.

Road widening at
Three Lamps.
How the embankment
was cut back to make
way for another lane.
(Mike Leigh, BRO)

The 'traffic measures' scheme was now so reduced that it fell into a 'permitted development' category, which did not require a public enquiry. Much of it will be familiar to current Totterdown residents. The Bath Road approach from Angers Road to Three Lamps and on down to Temple Meads would be widened to two lanes. A slip road to go up the Wells Road at Three Lamps would be provided. (The old corner of Totterdown which protruded between the Bath and Wells Road and formerly had the pie-shaped Reinge Tobacconists shop – like Glasnost – on it was cut right back for this.)The embankment on the west side of the Bath Road at Three Lamps would be cut back, (taking away a portion of Higham and Vernon Streets' 'green' space resulting from demolition), and there would then be enlarged footways and the foot-bridge put in on the west side. (In fact this was only completed in 1992.) There would also be the locally requested pedestrian crossings; slip roads would be cut in from Belleview to Cambridge Street and St John's Lane to Bushy Park and Bushy Park's junction with the Wells Road would be closed off.

A widening improvement would be made to St John's Lane and the construction of a roundabout there with a new link from Oxford Street carried out. The bottom of Oxford Street would then be closed off. These were all postponed for financial reasons but were slowly put in place year by year. Improvements to the junctions of Angers Road and Stanley Hill with Bath Road were included in the housing associations' costs and had to be done straight away. Other proposals, such as to link Bushy Park with Knowle Road, had to be abandoned completely for reasons of cost. The grant deadline already mentioned was in view – £360,000 payable on land used in the scheme prior to 1974. To achieve it, it was necessary to work through many of the improvements before embarking on what Totterdown really wanted – houses, people and shops put back.

At the same time there was an interesting plan which never materialized. This was to lock the Avon and to lay out a wide area between the Bath Road and the river as attractive and functional parkland with considerable play and leisure potential; eg a riverside walk, sitting area, children's activities area, extensive landscaping, a viewing point and a footpath link over the river to the Avon Walkway (as St Philips Greenway was then called). Due consideration to the landscaping of the area should be given at an appropriate time, ran the original Freeman Fox and Partners Plan blurb. That plan was never realized. (6)

A 2006 view of the 'proposed wide area for recreation' which came to nothing. Rebuilt middle Totterdown is seen behind it. (Kate Pollard)

The end of the road – LUTS

Following the local government re-organisation, the LUTS Report for 1973-86 had at last been published. It projected future pollution, car use, public transport and environmental impact; it recommended 'car user restraint policies' for rush hours – a cordon of toll booths around the City Centre – with priority given to public transport and Park and Ride schemes. It also proposed a new bus station; this was begun in 2005/6. It had militated against the new Parkway link to Montpelier but it had underlined the need for the Outer Circuit Road to be built to Totterdown to justify the time and public money already spent, and the demolition and evacuation that had taken place.

The Report had been launched in the local press, exhibited at the Planning Office and there had been local meetings and questionnaires in the *Evening Post*. LUTS Public information Meetings had been held in Knowle and Bedminster – but not in Totterdown. In an interesting rehearsal of its being raised again in the early 2000s, the proposed toll system had been well discussed and the majority of respondents had been against it. Instigated by LUTS, initial surveys for a Bristol Metro System had been begun. (Disappointingly both for the environment and Bristolians, the Metro plan has not been realised in the 30 years since.)

In 1980, with the Totterdown revised and reduced cost traffic solution described at Three Lamps worked out and underway, the City and County Councils were able to set about reparation work in Totterdown, which was to prove to be another tortuous process of finance crunching and manipulation of resources. Redevelopment and rebuilding were rather more radical and expensive than the Housing Action Area strategies which had already been underway on the Pylle area for four years by then.

Housing Action Area grants

In 1976 both Councils' Committees began to work on a Blight-busting strategy to improve Totterdown's existing residential and business area and consider how best to use the 'surplus' land in the future. Bristol City Housing was preparing a local scheme for Totterdown's revival, soon to be made public. Existing property was to be improved and elderly people's flats were planned; nursery places would be extended and so would the school.

In the first wave of it, more than 219 'substandard' owner-occupied, tenanted or let houses in St Luke's Road, Pylle Hill Crescent, Richmond Street and Clifton View, were targeted. 171 of them were brought 'up to standard' while families were temporaily rehoused 'which will ensure the long-term future of the area' as the Bristol Council's programme predicted. (7) Redland and Solon SW Housing Associations were brought in to carry out work on their existing houses and could negotiate to buy other dwellings to add to their social housing stock. By the end of this 5-year project, Redland owned 77 houses in and adjoining the Action Area.

Nigel Hall was their freelance architect for this work. Redland Housing Association had just been set up and this was their first major job. (8) Nigel designed repairs and improvements to many substandard Redland houses in those roads and during this period, Solon renovated some of the remaining houses on St Luke's Road as a hostel for the displaced.

The official hub of the Action Area was the Housing Advice Centre at 34 Pylle Hill Crescent where a Housing Officer and two surveyors were available to arrange temporary accommodation and liaise with building associations to provide the loans to householders against the cost of work on their properties. Grants were as well applied for and dealt with there. The Housing Associations' Working Group met there and it was an enquiry centre for the wider Totterdown too. Local groups, (including TAG), used it for meetings. House renovation grants became available when the Housing Action Area was widened beyond its original target area. The Advice Centre doubled as a small community centre.

There was also a Show House in Richmond Street which demonstrated what could be done with a House Renovation Grant. 'You may not realise but 50 per cent grants (or in a Housing Action Area), 75 per cent grants are available,' wrote Councillor Chris Reid invitingly. (9)

Nigel's archive shows that he designed for a cross-section of work, including conversions to flats, demolition of outhouses and damaged walls, roof and many ceiling repairs – although the walls of hilly Totterdown houses are flexible, their ceilings are not; polystyrene-tiled ceilings were fashionable at the time but highly inflammable, so many were removed. Kitchens and bathrooms were modernised; window and doorframes were repaired. The balance of grants could be provided by a 10-45 per cent mortgage and Abbey National were on hand at the Advice Centre.

In a neat bit of symmetry, a public meeting to launch and explain the housing action area plans, opened by Councillor Graham Robertson, Chair of Bristol City Council's Housing Committee, was held in the Wycliffe Congregational Chapel on the corner of Windsor Terrace, St Luke's Crescent and St Luke's Road in October 1976. In 1978 the Chapel itself closed for its own reasons following Rev Malcolm Shapland's last sermon there. Nowadays of course the handsome building would be converted but this was not the policy of the time which was to rebuild with clean, un-

The former Wycliffe Congregational Chapel on the corner of Windsor Terrace and St Luke's Crescent. (Nigel Hall)

Wycliffe Row in 2006, architected by Nigel Hall, seen from St Luke's Road. (Kate Pollard)

decorative lines. It was demolished and Redland Housing Association commissioned Nigel Hall to design some 'new build' homes on its site.

By 1981, Cyril Fortune, Director of Housing, reported back on the first wave of the project: the problems on Pylle Hill had been compounded by the age and income levels of some of the house owners. The density of the housing and inadequacy of garden space and lack of rear access did not comply with 1981 standards. There had been a plan a few years earlier to

1985 saw Totterdown people petitioning Avon to remove the 'tinkers' from the area. Note 'tinkers' in the background. (BEP)

carry out some demolition and create 'breathing spaces' but this was abandoned for obvious reasons. Environmental improvements had been made to St Luke's Steps and to the narrow paths at the back of some rows; pavements in St Luke's Crescent and elsewhere were repaired. (10) Interest in new ownership had increased and young people were moving into the area.

Repair and improvement grants were extended to other parts of Pylle Hill and Totterdown and by then legislation had made it necessary to flood areas with explanatory newsletters. This was in 1982 when Clive Clifford acquired his grant for around £12,000. He remembers the beautiful white folder with a picture of Totterdown which contained your information.

From 1976 to the mid 1980s, Housing Action on existing houses was taking place across Totterdown. In 1988 a resident newly arrived in Totterdown from Somerset wrote: 'The availability of Council grants meant that for the first year I was here, there didn't seem to be any street without at least three sets of scaffolding. The second year saw the scaffolding being replaced by For Sale signs in every street and house prices soaring. I just hope this doesn't mean an invasion of yuppies as Bristol booms'. (11)

It was a similar concern that gave rise to the anonymous Totterdown Rap.

Totterdown Rap (for aspiring first time buyers)

It's the Totterdown rap man the Totterdown rap.

Totterdown is where it's at!

Family pub, disappearing cats,

Streets of skips and yuppie twits

They'll clear away the cemetery caskets

And build more houses with hanging baskets

With their Barbour wax and the Brown Brogues too

The yuppies are here and they're after you! etc (12)

More money gets juggled...

In 1980, the aftermath in the centre of Totterdown where once 2,000 people had lived, and where most of the businesses and their owners had been removed, was a wasteland scattered with gypsies, tinkers, horses, vans, rubbish, dumped cars, and so on. They were still there in 1985 when 266 Totterdown people petitioned for their permanent removal from the site and Bushy Park because of squalor, intimidation, noise, theft and hygene problems. (13) This is the poisoned chalice which Bill Graves, new Head of Avon County Council had inherited.

He made a statement on behalf of Avon which was the prelude to 12 years of redevelopment of the 20-acre 'Core Site' as it was now designated. Graves predicted that the land be developed by housing associations and co-operatives and plus possibly some private developers. The unspoken rationale for the latter was that this had to go some way towards subsidising the housing, which was to serve a social aim. (14)

The alacrity with which Avon suddenly jumped to it and brought all the various parties together to make it happen is notable. There is no hint in the records to show whether it was fuelled by sympathy, alarm or horror at what the attitudes of the last 14 years ago had perpetrated. There was still the matter of some more road juggling, involving the closure of New Walls Road and County Street against the Bath Road, and the establishment of the Wells Road/Angers Road entrance to the site, to qualify the release of the Core Site for redevelopment to qualify for a land grant – now apparently worth a hefty £2.3m. On the other hand, road improvements money had been nearly halved. There is no question that the County Council pursued every grant and private subsidy and every partnership it could arrange in order to achieve the redevelopment of the Core Site.

7 The Zone Jigsaw

Totterdown was once again in jeopardy. Just as the deal was struck, the Government firmly turned off the tap of funds to housing associations.
Councillor Pam Tatlow

Totterdown's Core Site was divided into zones on a plan, with different types of housing or commercial developments allocated to each one. In 1983 the plans were in the hands of a special Totterdown Redevelopment Scheme Committee which contained personnel from Avon, including County Architects and Treasury; Social Services, Planning and Legal Services; Bristol City Council representatives headed by George Micklewright and the City Planners; delegates from housing associations including, (at this stage), the United Kingdom Housing Trust, a housing association consultant and Bristol Churches Housing Association.

The Housing Associations were to buy the land and obtain planning permission from the Council to build on it. The Housing Associations had a consortium of funders; they also had subsidiaries; so there are a great number of interests and agendas tied up in this site. The 'opening' Housing Association, UKHT together with its subsidiaries had become Kingdomwide Ltd by 1984. The County Architect was still proceeding with land acquisition from the Totterdown stalwarts who'd refused to move, by the means of compulsory purchase. Social Services' brief was to provide 30-35 'units' of housing for elderly people on Bushy Park, with a communal room for 'helping' other elderly people in the area. The development on Bushy Park fulfilled the social housing criteria but would also raise capital for the Core Site.

TAG considered Iain Patterson even-handed but as he was Head of City Planning and not part of the Avon Highways Department he could not influence overall the proposed rebuilding; George Micklewright was a member of the Housing Committee in time to bring the Housing Associations into the redevelopment. Although Kingdomwide came in for much criticism, TAG recognised it offered the only opportunity for the badly needed rebuilding programme.

Council Planning pointed out that 'some difficulty would be the sloping nature of the terrain' in case delegates hadn't noticed that Totterdown was on a hill. The County architect anticipated the need for a noise barrier 'towards the Wells and possibly Bath Roads'. Everybody with a stake in the redevelopment expressed their ability to procure the necessary funds to get started. There was anxiety over the commercial development of the prime parts of the site, as it left everyone else with what were perceived as the less desirable parts.

Compulsory purchase got underway again where pink appeared on the new plan for Stanley Hill, Highgrove Street (where the heroic Mr Bradbeer had hung on in there at number 22 for a further decade), County Street, Oxford Street, (presumably what had been named by the locals 'Oxford Street Stop and Go') and St John's Lane. Many owners were unwilling or could not be found. In view of the fact that the site was about to rebuilt, one could wonder why more demolition was thought to be necessary.

Totterdown Redevelopment meeting at the YMCA with (L) Iain Patterson, City Planning Officer with Councillor Richards (R), Councillor Chris Reid, (Centre), Chair of TAG, Pam Stephens, Secretary of TAG, and Councillor David Poole. (BEP)

This was the team initially set up to put Totterdown to rights and to expel the last evacuees. From then on, ad hoc committees carried on the business. A public meeting was held in Totterdown to publicise the plan and the Housing Associations' proposals were well received. Residents also had a say in the widening of pavements and positioning of bus stops on Bath Road. Much of the incoming finance hung on the capital investors who

More Zoning plans, possibly at the same meeting. Councillor Pam Tatlow and Councillor David White inspect. (BEP)

had commercial advisors in their employ who called the shots. From then the juggling took on a new significance.

There had been from the start a Council recommendation for a community centre in Totterdown. In Feb 1981, the site of the previous 16-64 Wells Road, (Zone N), was under consideration for this. Later on there was a plan for Kingdomwide to construct one on part of the pub site. Sadly this was ruled out by events.

Extending the shopping area became a stumbling block. Totterdown people wanted it in

Sapling planting has begun. (BEP)

Commercial Barrington Court was built first to help finance the rest of the development. (Mike Leigh, BRO)

the one configuration, where their shops had previously been; the commercial planners wanted to site them 'more commercially'. The Council had to arbitrate. A new pub was central to the plan, but getting this in the wrong place could generate public protest, worried the Council, now sensitive to protest. Breweries had yet to be contacted; the Council wanted to move the pub from the developers' choice for it, Zone N, because Zone N (the Council thought) would be more suitable for 'community facilities'. Moxley Jenner for the Developers said irritatedly that if the pub site were to be moved, their whole plan would have to be redesigned.

The Council worried that the shops placed where Totterdown people wanted them 'would not generate enough value to contribute to the housing development'. The UK Housing Trust had been involved in these negotiations. By 1984 this impasse had reached its zenith and after years of argument, in and out of the Chamber, Councillor Andy May gave his undertaking to: 'ensure that the advice, particularly in respect of the pub, would be carefully and comprehensively worded to assist the general public. The developers would also be given precise information as to the views expressed by local people.' (1) The UK Housing Trust had later obtained their own commercial advice on the siting of the shops and the pub and were prepared to re-site the pub on the opposite side of the road. The pub was the new Bush, which eventually ended up on today's site. The Council Officers were happy with this and Kingdomwide were then able to proceed with their plans to develop Bushy Park. Their next step was to purchase it and then enter into a development agreement with Avon.

The shops and pub site had to be sold to raise capital and the shops didn't turn out to be what

Development begins on Bushy Park in the mid 1980s. (BEP)

everyone had in mind. Kingdomwide had asked the Government for an Urban Development grant. The Government had said that house prices had gone up so much, that the Totterdown site was commercially viable and should pay for itself. This was the turned off tap that Pam Tatlow had referred to. This led to huge compromises having to be made and pragmatism all round at not achieving what the Committees had first set out to achieve. (2)

The redevelopment machinations would fill a book on their own but the following snapshot of its problems and manipulations will provide some insight. The whole process was agonisingly slow; planning permission was long drawn out and housing associations and Social Services successively withdrew from the field for their own domestic reasons. Other trusts moved in (eg. the Sutton Trust which took over the elderly people's provision and whose building development, Bush Court, is there today). Money got shifted about, zones changed, housing units changed with the developing climate of the 1980s. The development work very gradually fell into place after which bushy landscape and trees were added.

The houses and apartments were built according to the regulations of the 1980s with respect to inside and outside space and internal natural light. They were built in brick and there was an attempt to design them in the manner of the local architecture, but the modern 1980s regulations made this impossible. They were underpinned, unornamented and largely built in groups instead of terraces. They were very different from ornamented Victorian Totterdown with its high density terraces straddling impossible gradients.

Nigel Hall's terraced row design on Highgrove Street tried to come closer to Totterdown architecture. There are also some better-matched short terraces facing each other inside the

Three Lamps development-to-be around 1990. (Mike Leigh, BRO)

Iron girders for Dillons (now Tescos) being put in place in the mid 1980s. (BEP)

Work on the New Bush pub also beginning, mid 80s. (Mike Leigh, BRO)

site, architected by Solon. Although Three Lamps Development is in architectural contrast to its surroundings, because of its wonderful landscaping it could in the opinion of the writer be likened to a modern day garden city layout.

From the start there was little 'social housing' on Three Lamps Development. It was, and is, mostly in shared ownership – to help young people get onto the housing ladder. Margaret Dudbridge, a former evacuee from the first Angers Road, returned from Hartcliffe with her husband Jim to Totterdown's Stevens Crescent as soon as they could. Jim had enquired at the Estate Agents as to whether they could buy a house on the new housing development. He was told firmly that they were 'not for Totterdown people'. Jim's experience may have been a common one.

8 A Tribute to Some of the Positive Legacies

After the recent onslaught on Totterdown the community is determined to put itself back on the map by holding a 3-day celebration.
Bush Telegraph

We don't need to get maudlin here about the cohesiveness of the local community. However, there is a surviving legacy of some small places, features or groups which were set up, acquired from or just survived Totterdown's demolition and blighted period. In the writer's opinion, their origins should not be forgotten and they should be designated as local icons.

The Totterdown Centre

This re-used the well-loved Harris and Tozer draper' shop – a good gesture in itself – the shop from which corsets were sent home on approval. It was bought by John Grimshaw, Sue Learner and a newly-formed Co-operative and limited company who turned it into the 'Totterdown Shopping, Community Action and Exhibition Centre' with aspirational aims. This development was a huge altruistic gesture to Totterdown to help it through bad times. Although the building no longer operates as a Centre, a number of groups which started life in it, remain and flourish.

The front and side of the Totterdown Centre building were painted up in a geometric design by Bristol University and Art College students and in 1979 the Centre opened its doors to the Totterdown public to provide the named shopping, community action and exhibitions. Tony Benn, then Minister for Energy, carried out the opening ceremony. He was presented with a sweater knitted by the Centre's machine knitting group complete with a BENN SAVES IT! logo. Sue Learner remembers that the logo was largely obscured as Benn turned out to be quite a bit larger than his sweater. Brenda Spriggs remembers the Centre's opening day: 'It was absolutely heaving – completely full. You couldn't move in there the day it opened.' She remembers the Centre stalls – (her daughter worked on one selling jewellery on a Saturday). 'Mum and I used to go down shopping and go to the café'; also to the Grain Store because her mum liked muesli.

John Grimshaw's reminisced about the origins of the Totterdown Centre: 'When the demolition was going on a group got together who said, we've really got to draw a line somewhere. The Drapers had been driven out of business so a group came together to run the wholefood, a tool shop and restaurant. Right from the beginning we had the Children's

The Totterdown Centre is opened by constituency MP Tony Benn. Note the band on the roof, poised to play. (BEP)

Workshop as we wanted part of the building to be of benefit to the community. In parallel with that, I was starting off the cycling group which took over full time, so Sue managed the Centre.' John's cycling group developed the local and first walkway path – the St Philips Greenway, accessible from May Walk on the opposite side of the river and leading to Sparke Evans Park.

Two years after opening, the Centre's fixtures and activities had expanded to include the Children's Workshop, the Advice Centre and Good Neighbours' Scheme; Traders, Reg and Brenda's Fruit & Veg, shoe repairs and key-cutting and woollen goods with a resident machinist. Practical projects included the Alternative Technology Centre and the Street Warden and Street Fixer Scheme, operating out in the community; also the screws, nails and insulation shop. The Bike Workshop and the Totterdown Women's (Woodworking) Workshop were other practical projects. A local handiwork stall, a haberdashery, a picture frames shop, an Oxfam, fancy goods, pet-foods, and book stalls spiced up the variety. The Grain Store and Poppies Restaurant were central to the social and food life and added to the shopping factor.

Exhibitions over that year included, (of course) the proposed road scheme; the work of St Peter's Hospice, the Samaritans, La Leche League, Friends of the Earth, the Youth Opportunities Centre, Knowle Junior School, (now Hillcrest), the Richmond Fellowship, Tools for Self Reliance, (tools were collected at the Centre and sent to developing countries). Work by the resident Totterdown Centre artists was also on display, including their painting, pottery, needlework and silk screen printing. They had created an outside mural, posters for the Festival, and Totterdown Centre Christmas cards and led arts workshops. There were Wednesday teas for the elderly and also a resident band which played at the Totterdown Festival. The meeting room and kitchen could be hired.

This very much fulfilled the Co-operative's objectives and put back a heart, beating with 1970s aspirations, into desolate Totterdown. However, it had its opponents from the beginning – John again: 'We had opposition locally and from the Action Group because we were part commercial. We actually *lost* funds because they wrote to our funding body to complain about this. TAG had no time for the businesses.'

This local chill was demonstrated in an article by Councillor Chris Reid in *Bush Telegraph*: 'I hear that plans are afoot for the development of Harris & Tozers' former shop by business people in the name of the

The Totterdown Centre's Cycle Workshop; Roger Ferns doing repairs on Christopher and young Tom Orlik's bike. (BEP)

community. I would welcome a co-operative; Totterdown people working at a venture for mutual good would be useful indeed!' Although it ignored the altruism, (eg the management group funded the foundation of the Children's workshop themselves), TAG was concerned that downtrodden and demoralised locals should participate in the Centre's running.

Antagonism both within and without the Centre was a hindrance and this eventually unravelled the Co-operative. When the Totterdown Centre Co-operative finally broke up, the core of the Centre did the same. Fortunately, Sue Learner remained the owner of the Children's Workshop building. The Children's Community Workshop and the Women's Workshop remain and are very successful symbol of those early aspirations. Some Centre stalwarts – the greengrocers, the Grain Store and Poppies Restaurant remained open for a

January 1990: Totterdown Women's Workshop received funding support from the Government Inner Area Programme towards its training for women in woodwork, plumbing and renovation. (BEP)

good few years after that – Bob and Brenda's Fruit & Veg until around 2003. Nowadays sections of the building are held by five main 999-year lease remainder holders. They are Bob the former Grocer, the Women's Workshop; the Children's Workshop; added to them is the commercial section – currently a Chinese take-away and a property letting business.

The Totterdown Centre was an icon of the times and the Children's Community Workshop and the Women's Workshop continuing ones. John Grimshaw's and Sue Learner's community efforts in what was a difficult climate were appreciated by many; this was the first attempt to set up a community centre in Totterdown. The cycling element developed and over the years led to the formation of Cyclebag and eventually SUSTRANS (Sustainable Transport). The common denominator was John Grimshaw; the St Philips Greenway path led on to the eventual making by volunteers of the Bristol to Bath Cyclepath, opened in 1986; this in turn eventually led to SUSTRANS' 10,000 miles of cycle network across the country.

The Women's Workshop in the Totterdown Centre

Teaching woodwork and upholstery skills, it had been set up in 1981 as a charity by Anne Harding. It offered a Craft and Design Course, which was an off-shoot from Redland College. Numbers of its members had passed 3000 several years ago at which the Workshop stopped counting. It is now self-supporting. Anne guesses that there are wooden items which were made in it all over Bristol. Nowadays its classes meet three evenings a week. Members came originally from all ethic minorities, possibly because it was then grant-aided. It has such a longstanding reputation that Students mostly join the Workshop through word of mouth. This is another continuing icon with arguably the bests ign in Totterdown.

The Totterdown Children's workshop in the Totterdown Centre

'Funding has always been a nightmare,' Paul Dielhelm, the Co-ordinator at the time, wrote of the work to keep the Workshop running; in 1980 it was threatened with closure because of the Rates bills. However, in the 1990s, the music benefits and events which supported it were the high spots of the Totterdown social calendar. Filling it to capacity has never been a problem. It offers creative play and activities, arts and visits to places children wouldn't otherwise go to. The photos tell the story. In present times it has raised the game of its annual auction, a local, must-go-to, truly creative event. At the time of writing, the Children's workshop is full, iconic and still central to the lives of many of Totterdown's current generation of young families. (1)

Catering workers at Quadrant raised the funds for this new Children's Workshop sign, *top*. (BEP)

By 1992, there were 70 children registered. (BEP)

Zone N (Where the Nat West Bank and the Bush Hotel once stood)

The name 'Zone N' survives from Avon's Redevelopment Plan. The 1983 Planning Brief hoped: 'that the site designated for community use will allow for the construction of a community centre when resources can be found by the local community.' As it turned out, the community took possession of another zone instead and Zone N was turned into a hilly hedge- screened park beside the former YMCA building, as described below. As it hasn't yet been given its own name – and this may happen in the future – it is known locally as 'the Pigeon Park' or 'the Park by the Phone Box'.

In the years between demolition and redevelopment the whole Bushy Park site was levelled and grassed over and then became a very well used stretch of 'community park' right in Totterdown's centre. Its position was ideal for the surrounding buildings. The Methodist Church Youth Club and the YMCA's youth clubs played football on it. The Methodist Young Wives group ran pancake races there. There were big community bonfires and fireworks organised by the Festival group. Some of the Road Protest activities took place there and – perhaps most memorably – the Totterdown Festival Carnival gathered on it to have its floats and costumes judged by the Lord Mayor or other dignitaries before parading around

Totterdown. This continued until the streets of Totterdown, (the parade visited all of them), was lined with parked cars and the floats couldn't get through.

These activities were made smaller scale by the building redevelopment. A portion of the land – Zone N – became a dedicated park. This was down to Ruth Brown and other members of TCA (Totterdown Community Association) who had serious concerns over the state of Zone N which had a shambolic and unhygenic travellers' lorry encampment. Ruth took part in TCA's consultation over Zone N's problems door to door around Totterdown and took back its findings to Avon. The unanimous outcome of the survey was to rid the site of the travellers as there were south Bristol sites set up for them and landscape it as a park for the community to use in such a way that travellers would be unable to return. There was swift agreement from Avon County Council and the landscaping was carried out very soon afterwards. To prevent the travellers' return, a hill was created and shrubs were planted round its borders. Nowadays they are mature and it is well-screened from the three surrounding busy roads. The hill is still there. Zone N is not used so much by groups although apparently the Methodist Church did bring out a Good Friday congregation for a service there at some time in the past. At the time of writing, Zone N is threatened by a developer; local people are trying to maintain it as a community green space. Its future is uncertain but any part of Totterdown which is a remaining 'zone' deserves icon-hood.

Zone A

Looking at the Zone A land confirms that Totterdown builders had developed 'high density' into an artform as there had formerly been thirteen buildings/fourteen businesses. on the site. Zone A remains as open space and a wildflower meadow has been created on it. The land belongs to the community under the stewardship of TACA (Totterdown Area Community Association). TACA grew from TCA and was constituted in 1986 and has carried out community work across the locality for 15 years.

TACA's relationship with Zone A began in 1989. After prolonged negotiations, it acquired the land's freehold from Avon County Council on behalf of the community. Zone A was to have been developed by a Nazarene Church which then opted to go elsewhere. TACA's first constitutional aim was to develop a community centre in Totterdown and Avon wanted a community centre built not by themselves but by another party, so Zone A was agreed by both parties to be the best site. TACA then spent many years of planning and fundraising for various aspirational arts and community centres. It ran events on the site, such as the memorable 1992 Zone A Day festival and the surviving paved stage dates back to that event. Zone A Day was successfully repeated in 1994. Both were good fund-raisers; they showed,

Negotiating Zone A for the community: Sue Mayer puts a point to Councillors David White and Tom Turvey of the City's Property Services. Vivien Pipping is on the far right at the back. (BEP)

Landscaping Zone N in the late 1980s following local consultation. (BEP)

too, that the site could become a successful outdoor community activities area very well. By the early 1990s – which were the height of the resident bands and Music Project era in Totterdown – much of TACA's local fundraising enterprises centred on 'home grown' music. Applications to funding sources were also made.

In 1995 TACA drew up a detailed preliminary plan for a Zone A wildflower garden, planting, seating, bonfire pit, ball-game area, stage and sculpture sites for daylight hours use; it waited until its commissioned Community Profile (the first of many) was complete, to 'test the water' in Totterdown. In 1996 some initial funding had been acquired for this 'al fresco centre' plan and TACA commissioned a Feasibility and Consultation study, visiting all relevant groups and organisations to 'Plan for Real' what Totterdown people wanted on Zone A.

1994, and TACA publicises acquiring Zone A for the community. (BEP)

The 2002 result from this was a far more developed plan, which was then approved for a 'Doorstep Green' funding application. Zone A's future seemed at last decided and affordable to everybody's satisfaction.

Although according to the early covenant, Zone A cannot be sold commercially because of its community designation, it was necessary to protect it and three TACA Members took on Zone A's official Trusteeship after a search lasting from 1997-2002.

Meanwhile, across the Wells Road in 2002 Totterdown, the YMCA building was to change hands and the institutional and community meeting space it had provided until then was under threat. An action group formed to campaign against this loss and when the YMCA was sold anyway, the group turned its attention to Zone A which it believed should instead become the site of a new build community centre. The protest group became the single-purpose TNCCG (Totterdown Neighbourhood Community Centre Group).

TACA by this time had now been awarded £60,000 with which to develop the 'Doorstep Green' design for Zone A. This would include the creation of the Green and 3 years of subsequent maintenance. TNCCG believed that the land would be 'tied up' for 25 years which was anathema to them. They were against TACA's suggestion that TNCCG develop another vacant building in Totterdown instead, because they were very confident of raising £1.5m funding for new a purpose-built Centre. They circulated a leaflet throughout Totterdown to promote their alternative plan for a community centre building. In order for them to proceed, TACA and its grant had to be neutralised by any means and TNCCG to this end carried out a hostile take-over. In 2004, TACA and TNCCG agreed to further local consultation on the matter of Zone A and an impartial Totterdown-wide survey was organized and carried out by the South Bristol Community Worker. This gave all residents the choice to vote for the Doorstep Green or a projected community centre. The result came back at 299 to 231 in favour of the community centre proposal.

TACA returned its £60,000 grant and at TNCCG's suggestion, agreed in April 2004 to lease Zone A to them for a period of three years, that being the time TNCCG needed to raise the funding to build and start the Centre.

Two and a half years down the line, TNCCG have commissioned a business plan and architect's design for the community centre and applied successfully for planning permission. So far the £1.5m has not been achieved but it is a case of 'Watch this Space', literally. Zone A is a 'work in progress' icon. (2)

Zone A Day poster.

Totterdown Festival and Carnival

This Festival was a fun event central to Totterdown people's lives during the demolition years, it kept their spirits up and is still fondly remembered. It has therefore achieved icon designation in this section.

It began in 1973 when the Minister of the Methodist Church wrote in *Bush Telegraph*: 'After the recent onslaught on Totterdown the community is determined to put itself back on the map by holding a 3-day celebration on 5/6/7 October.' Enthusiasm was immediately generated and a Carnival Parade gathered on Bushy Park that year and judging of costumes and floats was attended to by the *Bristol Evening Post* Kids' Page editor and Radio Bristol. Up at the school, there were exhibitions and there was a Festival Concert. There were also sports events which took place on Bushy Park.

Thereafter there was an annual Totterdown Festival AGM at which ideas and plans for the next one were mooted and survival plans discussed. 'Still the people of TD quite rightly are calling for more community facilities...the question: Where do we go from here will be exercising some of our minds at the AGM.' wrote the Minister. (3)

In January 1975 Totterdown people were invited to watch a film of the Festival at Holy

The original Totterdowners at the 1978 Carnival. (BEP)

Lord Mayor of Bristol, Councillor Ted Wright, waves to floats that he has, no doubt, just judged. (BEP)

Nativity Church and raise suggestions for the next one. The Carnival was the most memorable part of the event engendering great enthusiasm for costume-making. Brenda Spriggs remembers a particular fondness for gypsies and the Diddy Men. Sue Learner recalls the Totterdown Centre creating a carnival float with a replica Three Lamps sign on it. These always set off from and returned to Bushy Park amid a large gathering. Jean Piper and family were involved every year and Jean provided the description which follows. Every

Punks at the 1985 Carnival – sisters Sherrie and Kelly Groves and Nicky Davey. (BEP)

organisation and many streets set up a prefabricated tableaux which were transferred onto borrowed flatbed lorries brought to Bushy Park just before the procession began. Many featured scenery painted by local artists. There was also a walking procession, fancy dressed individuals and small groups which were often unprogrammed so they could be surprise items. The cavalcade, lorries and all, then processed round all the streets in Totterdown.

Most years there was a lamb roast on the Green following the carnival cooked by Pete Williams, the baker (the spit is still stored in the church cellar). There were also sports and for several years a tug-of-war – mainly an inter-pubs contest. There was a Hells Angels' team (the Totterdown Chapter was based until recently on Knowle Road). The Angels were also represented on the Festival Committee which was diversely also composed of the Baptist and Holy Nativity Churches, the Mosque and Totterdown Traders.

We can follow the Festival through until the Fingerpost Issue 6th Dec in 1988. It had evidently been a 9-day event for several years but in 1988 was shortened to a 2-day event again. It appears that the Festival organisers had been the organisers of other activities on the Green as well, e.g. theNovember 5th bonfires and fireworks parties. We run out of information about the Festival after 1988, its last year in action after running for fifteen. Its end was brought by the increasing numbers of parked cars lining the streets which prevented the floats processing round them. Without the Carnival procession there could be no Festival. The Totterdown Festival had flourished and brought creative energy back into Totterdown during its dismal days in the area. It is definitely an icon.

Peter Wright making sure the precious Three Lamps Sign is being carefully craned into place. (Peter and Pat Wright)

The Three Lamps Fingerpost

This signpost is so integral to people's consciousness in Totterdown that it has been used by many local groups as an emblem and by the Totterdown Music Project, and then by TACA, as a name for a newsletter. It was a grimly symbolic moment when it was removed just before demolition began and its reinstatement and refurbishment was a celebration of the return to normality when the Road threat to Totterdown was removed. This part of its story has already been told in Chapters 2 and 3.

Twenty one feet tall and made of cast iron it weighs 2.8 tons. It was originally instated at the Bath and Wells Road Junction in 1830. It was one of a series of improvements made to the Bath Road, around the same time, all the work of the local Turnpike Trust. The Trust was particularly advanced as it had been one of the first to have its working practices overhauled by the road engineer McAdam who lived in Bristol. The Bath Road was the first McAdamised road ever. (4) Under the same Turnpike Trust the Bath Road entering Totterdown was in 1833 'straightened and widened, part of Pylle Hill being cut away to ease the gradients'. (5) It may have changed its position slightly at that time because of that road alteration but there is no record of this. It certainly changed its position when it was reinstated because of the next alterations made to the junction. Re-erecting it in July 1983 after its refurb in Totterdown by the local Peter Wright Engineering Company was a major task requiring a flatbed lorry with a crane to lower it on to its purpose-built brick plinth. Several companies were needed for the work; they also brought along their friends and Totterdown people turned out to watch. It was a heart-warming occasion.

Originally equipped with gas lighting, it was fitted with electric lamps in the following year following a request from the Civic Society. Ronald Cleeves wrote in the *Post* at that time that his mother had told him that when she was a child the Three Lamps sign marked the end of public lighting – there were no more lamps up the Wells or Bath Roads.

With a repossession story, a symbolistic history and affection rating of that nature, the Three Lamps Signpost story designates it a top icon.

9 Some Last Words on Various Matters

That Chancery Fund

As we have explained earlier, there were a number of absentee house owners on whom the Council attempted to serve Compulsory Purchase Orders. Their houses were demolished anyway but in about 1970 the Council lodged a sum in an 'Unclaimed Balances' fund in the Chancery Courts in London in case they reappeared. On production of proof of ownership, they or their successors could have applied to become beneficiaries of the fund.

The writer has been involved in correspondence since April 2005 with Bristol City Council's Solicitor's Department which disclosed that it had no knowledge of the Fund but would investigate and should it still exist, 'consideration of your request to ring-fence this money for the Totterdown area will be given once the amount remaining has been ascertained and the likelihood of future possible claims has been assessed'. In July 2006 came the news that there was approximately £43,000 of money still intact at the Courts Fund Office, then in August, that most of it had been paid out to beneficiaries.

On 27 September 2006 the writer again rang the Chancery Officer and also emailed the Council's Solicitors' Office, hoping for the promised but un-received update. The Chancery Officer said that there is a live 'list' and balance accounts and that the Fund Officer prompts and updates the Councils involved annually; that it's down to the Council which made the original lodgement to make a re-claim and then use the fund residue as it sees fit; that the Councils in question keep scrupulous records of funds and beneficiaries.

Although there was an enthusiastic response from our Council Solicitors' Office back in April 2005 it was subsequently made clear that it was the Council's/Councillors' decision where they directed the fund residue. You can cook up all sorts of conspiracy theories about this Chancery fund and whether and when it has returned to Bristol, but this is a history book and we're reporting the facts. They are pretty changeable and enigmatic and yes, the writer doesn't follow them either! We hope some of the money has reached ex-Totterdowners. If so, and you are one, if you feel like it, please let us know!

Compulsory purchase of people's homes – it still happens!

Compulsory purchase, demolition and redevelopment of whole Victorian artisan areas, even in an age of sustainability and environmentalism and with the hindsight of the glaring redevelopment mistakes of the 1960s, surprisingly still appears to hold sway. At the time of writing, government-backed schemes to demolish and redevelop artisan areas of

Goole, Yorkshire (1) and the historic Welsh Streets in Toxteth, Liverpool (and not only because Ringo Starr grew up in one) (2) and in Bootle, Yorkshire (3) are underway, not for road building but, local protest groups claim, to solve social problems. Originally backed by John Prescott, there has been no local authority attempt to tackle problems any other way or to regenerate run-down housing stock other than by grant-aided demolition, land acquisition and re-housing. There appears to be little information available to anyone affected on the latter or indeed on the local authority motivation involved, so it is easy for anyone opposed (as many of the evictees are) to refer as Bootle at least, as an exercise in social cleansing. Much and also very little has changed since the 1960s.

A '60s Postscript from Adge Cutler

Totterdown could have been divided in two as Hotwells was after the building of the Cumberland Basin, (see the Cumberland Basin-style roads planned for Totterdown in Chapter 2). The traffic noise and pollution from it is constant and it's a kamikaze job crossing the Hotwells Road on foot. Here's Adge's tribute:

> *Hast seen our brand new bridge,*
> *Down there in Cumberland Basin?*
> *The cars go by like thunder,*
> *Up'n down and under,*
> *But where they goes*
> *Nobody knows*
> *It aint no flamin' wonder!*

A Final Analysis by ANON of Totterdown:

Totterdown Song

> *There was once a tumbling terrace, that everyone thought*
> *would perish. But instead of decay we've made it today,*
> *Into a Totterdown town that we cherish.*
> (*Finger Post* August 1988 p. 13)

A note about the Bristol Road Show

The show was mounted at the New Vic, 1972/73
Author: David Illingworth. Director: Howard Davies. Designer: Chris Dyer
Actors: Marcia King, Ian Marter, Michael Lewis, Paul Moriarty, Pete Postlethwaite
Anyone interested in visiting the Bristol Road Show can find it in the Bristol University

Theatre Collection. The Prompt Script is present together with a Ros Grimshaw cover design which was used for the posters. (4)

Song No 1, presumably by Illingworth, speaks for itself. Thanks to Bristol University Theatre Collection for access to this archive.

Bibliography

(All other publications used are listed fully in Chapter Notes, *below*)

Council Minutes have been bound into volumes without re-numbering and there are also multiple year volumes, all making referencing largely impossible. However, I have dated all relevant Council actions in the text and dates are the most useful reference points.

The Outer Circuit Road and Totterdown matters are minuted and demolition listed in BCC Planning and Traffic Committee Minute Books 1968-1972 at Bristol Record Office (BRO) After local government reorganisation, Totterdown/OCR matters are recorded from September 1974 in Avon P&HC (Planning and Highways Committee) 647 onwards also in ACC Land & Buildings volumes. The following had relevant information:

M/BCC/PTR/1/7 onwards.		1968-72	(Before local government reorganisation).
BRO A10051			(Following LGR)
ACC 650 L&B		1974/5	
ACC 655 L&B		1975/6	
ACC 457 L&B		1974/5	
ACC 663 L&B		1978/78	
ACC 665 L&B		1978/9	
ACC 665 P&HC		1977/77	
ACC 666 P&HC		1978/78	
ACC 667 P&HC		1979	
BCC & ACC/L&BC	1979	Joint Consultative Cttee	
ACC 552 P&HC		1979	
ACC 672 P&HC		1980	
ACC 675 P&HC	2 vols	1980	
ACC 676 P&HC		1980	

Totterdown Redevelopment 1981-7

ACC PH&T	3 vols	1981/2	
ACC 684 PH&T		1981/2	Totterdown District Plan
ACC 686 PH&T		1981/2	
ACC 687 PH&T		1982/2	Road improvements
ACC 688 PH&T		1982	

ACC 689 PH&T		1982/2	Totterdown options report
ACC 553 L&B		1983/4	More CPOs, core site
ACC 555 L&B		1983	
ACC 556 L&B		1983	CPOs, housing Assns etc
ACC 557 L&B		1983/4	Totterdown development consultation meeting
ACC 558-571L&B	14 vols	1984/1987	
ACC 696	3 vols	1983	Bath Rd
ACC 697 PH&T		1983/9	3 Lamps Junction
ACC 701 PH&T		1983/3	
ACC 702 PH&T	vol 2		
ACC 694 PH&T	vol 1	1983/4	

Chapter Notes

BEP = Bristol Evening Post
BRL = Bristol Reference Library
BRO = Bristol Record Office

Chapter 1

1. Janet and Derek Fisher, *Bygone Bristol: Totterdown and Knowle on old Postcards*, published by them in Bristol. Mike Hooper et al, Knowle and Totterdown, Archive Photography Series, Chalford 1996

2. Elsie Lawrance: *Growing up in Totterdown 1922-1936* p7 Redcliffe Press 1979

Chapter 2

1. Mary Wright, *Montpelier: A Bristol Suburb*, pp 111-114, Phillimore 2004. The book is very informational about the OCR protest as the Road would have radically affected Montpelier. David Hirschmann who galvanised the city-wide protest against the OCR lived in Montpelier at the time

2. BRO 42054. G Drawer

3. Tony Benn writing in the *Guardian* Nov 9th, 1963

4. Tony Benn writing in the *Guardian* May 15th 1964. Benn was opposition Spokesman on Transport in the early 1960s

5. David Starkie, *The Motorway Age: Road and Traffic Policies in Post-war Britain* p60, Pergamon Press 1982 p.60
BUL HE363.G7

6. David Starkie, *The Motorway Age* p71

7. *Ibid*

8. David Starkie, *The Motorway Age* p57

9. David Starkie, *The Motorway Age* p. 59

10. David Starkie, *The Motorway Age*. Only about one third of authorities had submitted traffic surveys by 1969, as required and these studies incorporated 'wildly incorrect, highly optimistic assumptions' on eg. population change, disposable incomes and car ownership p 68

11. David Starkie, *The Motorway Age* p73. '...death to house selling' is added by me, informed by friends' experiences at the time in Eastville!

12. David Starkie, *The Motorway Age* p77

13. BRO 35510 *Civic News* 94, Jan 1962 and 158, April 1966 describing the present and future policies in Totterdown. *Bristol Illustrated News* Jan 1966

14. Vivien later belonged to TAG, TCA and TACA developing many community initiatives in TACA

15. 'Oxford St Stop and Go' was a local joke which described the changing situation at the St John's Lane side of Oxford Street. The house owners were evicted; the properties were then part demolished then later, roofs were replaced, repairs made and they were let out to tenants. The houses were later cleared again and demolished. This was described by John and Paul Attwell, Vivien Pipping and Brenda Spriggs

Chapter 3

1. Bristol Council Planning and Traffic Committee Meetings Minutes see Bibliography

2. Re the route going anywhere, anytime, see Chapter 2 ref 15

3. The Men's Adult School was a similar instance of the building being bought up (for £1, 880) then re-let. (The closure of the School was also because it was less well-subscribed when access to mainstream education was widespread)

4. The Chancery Fund is described in the Introduction and updated at the beginning of Chapter 9

5. Westminster Bank is glimpsed in Plate 12 next to the Bush Hotel. In between and in front of them was a well-remembered fruit and veg stall – a permanent fixture. Other Bushy Park houses mentioned are shown in Plates 33 and 35

6. St Luke's Road, Cumberland Basin to Saint Luke's Railway Bridge: BEP 26 February 1963 BRL B32466; Remaining archaeology can be seen in Plate 39

7. BEP 5 June 1970 BRL B32466

8. *Ibid*

9. *Ibid* and BRO M/BCC/PTR/1/7

10. See Totterdown's Icons Chapter 8

11. *Civic News* 2, September 1957; Lawrence Hill and Easton were old and run down areas which provided 'a more convenient piece of land for redevelopment' ie the Road.

12. BEP 17 May 1972 BRL B28295

13. *Ibid*

14. Evident from 1984: PC&HC 647. The OCR was still on course as before but was on a back burner whilst Avon prioritised its funds

15. ACC 457. Estate Services was to negotiate the price in May 1974 but re-negotiation was decided against. He was finally paid off in February 1975

16. This is described in Chapter 3, 'Blight in Totterdown'

17. BEP 14 October 1972, 8 December 1972 and 29 December 1972, BRL B28295 – there was much press coverage of disgust, not only over the state Totterdown was in – which was disgusting and the pride local people had in the former order of Totterdown had been violated – but also at the attitude of the Council. At the 1972 meeting in Totterdown when the Council wanted to talk landscaping the meeting was closed when a Totterdown man shouted 'This is disgusting!' from the gallery

18. ACC P&HC 675 1980/81

19. Brenda Sprigg recalled bullying incidents relating to her children and the experience of neighbours

20. Totterdown's Three Lamps sign is described more fully in Chapter 8

Chapter 4

1. Architectural Design Vol 41 no 9, Sept pp 570

2. *Hitch Hiker's Guide to the Galaxy*, Douglas Adams, pp 11, 12. Pan Books

3. Council planners were enthusiastic about creating a new eclectic mix of old and new, see Bristol *Illustrated News*, January 1966, where the mix is still being promoted. In 1962 they had outlined the concept of the 'new, super suburb which revolved around skyscraper flats, a revolutionary shopping centre and the OCR – the city's 'inter-district freeway'

4. This is described by Elsie Lawrance writing about Totterdown between the wars, (ref Chapter 1, Note 2) which seems to have remained the status quo until people were evicted from Totterdown. Evictees found their new neighbourhoods to have (in comparison) un- neighbourly attitudes and a rapidly shifting population

5. See the first Angers Road in the Dedication

6. This is what the Council called all the demolition area when it drew up plans to redevelop it

7. See 3

8. *Bush Telegraph:* the Methodist Church's newsletter, January 1980, contained in its archive

9. BEP 6 February 1974, BRL B32466 and 8 December 1972 BRL

10. *Civic News* 122, July/Aug 68

11. *Civic News* 81, November 1964 in which it is propounded that a growing proportion of the urban population would want to be housed in multi-storey 'dwellings' because the popularity of the private garden had declined and by 1980 everyone would in any case own a car.
'Cathy Come Home' by Jeremy Sandford, influential BBC play about class and homelessness in 1966 directed by Ken Loach. Led almost immediately to the setting up of Shelter

12. This impetus was described as 'Clean Sweepism' which in 1953 architect Lance Wright identified and criticised in Bristol. Architects' Journal Vol 118 Sept 10th, p311

13. David Powell, *Tony Benn: A Political Life*, p.27 Continuum 2001

14. *Witness: A Blueprint for Survival* by Edward Goldsmith, Robert Allen helped by Michael Allaby, John Davoll, and Sam Lawrence. It was published in January 1972, occupying all of *The Ecologist* Vol. 2 No.1, in advance of the world's first ever Environment Summit, the 1972 UN Conference on the Human Environment, in Stockholm. So great was demand for the Blueprint that it was subsequently republished in paperback by Penguin books.

15. John V Punter, *Design Control in Bristol 1940-90* p.59 Redcliffe Press 1990

16. Described to me by Craig Begg and John Grimshaw

17. John Grimshaw's reminiscences in Chapter 5

18. John Grimshaw interviewed by Libby Purves on Radio 4's Midweek, 14 September 2005.

19. Mary Wright, *Montpelier: A Bristol Suburb*, Phillimore 2004. This process is described in her Decades of Protest Chapter 12 pp 114 onwards

20. Gerry Brooke's actions in keeping Totterdown in the news daily, contributed to the Totterdown

campaign which became direct action after he set up Totterdown Action Group, as he describes in his Preface. This also means that there is an extraordinary archive of photos at the Post and in scrapbook form in Bristol Central Library.

21. Mary Wright, *Montpelier* etc p 115

22. Decades of Protest. Shown in the evidence here re Totterdown

23. George Ferguson, *The 60s in Bristol*, p 27. Redcliffe Press.

24. BEP 11 April 1967 BRL B32466

25. BRL BL 17D: Gordon Priest and Pamela Cobb,*The Fight for Bristol* pp 69,70 Bristol Civic Society & Redcliffe Press 1980

26. *Ibid* and also Mary Wright, Montpelier, Decades of Protest p 115

27. BEP 8 December 1971 BRL B28295

28. Mary Wright: *Montpelier, Decades of Protest* p 115

29. BEP 18 February 1972 BRL B28295

30. BEP 6 October 1972 BRL B28295

David Illingworth appealed to Walker and Jenkins to attend the show and explain the proposed OCR to the people it affected. Unsurprisingly they did not. The 'group who staged the show' had hoped to get councillors and residents together to 'talk things out'. Two councillors did come along with Benn –Arthur Palmer and Roy Morris, who admitted that the Labour Group in Bristol had failed to stop the Road reaching Totterdown. (In June 1973, the Labour Group were to vote 18:15 in favour of proceeding with Stages 2 and 3.) Several audience members pointed out it was now 14 years too late. Shows that the Road Show was designed to challenge and invite debate – direct action, in fact.

31. The vigil took place while the Planners were meeting in the Council House, College Green. It included a torchlight procession through the areas affected by the Road plan – including Totterdown BEP 1 November 1970 BRL B28295

32. Mary Wright: *Montpelier, Decades of Protest* Chapter p 116; In fact the new 2-tier planning system was a recipe for conflict and confusion

33. BEP 9 June 1972 BRL B28295

34. BEP 19 July 1972 BRL B28295

Chapter 5

1. BEP 29 June 1972 BRL B28295. The tone of the article shows Jenkins has at least temporarily become one of the Good Guys over 'modification at Totterdown'; but then he backtracks confusingly to a if we can get the 75% grant for the Road, we'll go to Bedminster position on 10 July 1972

2. *Western Daily Press* 24 August 1972 BRL B28295 – ' a very acceptable solution to short term traffic difficulties' (Jenkins).

3. The Council believed (wrongly) that Totterdown would be appeased. (Incredulity factor as described in Chapter 4) BEP 9 June 1972 BRL B28295 .

4. BEP June 9th 1972 BRL B28295

5. *Bush Telegraph*, November 1997 Edition, p.5.

6. At the meeting noted in 3, 'A Totterdown and Lower Knowle Community Association was formed and Mr Chris Reid (spelt Reed) was elected Chair.' This may be one and the same as the Totterdown and Lower Knowle Tenants' Association listed below

7. Chris Reid, *Bush Telegraph* p 8, March 1978

8. BEP 12 June 1973 BRL B28295

9. Also mentioned by David Starkie in *The Motorway Age: Road and Traffic Policies in Postwar Britain* pp 68, 59 Pergamon Press 1982. The strategic transport studies used here had been imported from America. Authorities were using LUTS reports to build on development plans they already had.

10. See Chapter 8, The Totterdown Centre

11. BEP 8 December 1972 BRL B28295

12. This is a reminiscence contributed by Graham Davey; sadly we can't date it

13. BEP 3 January 1973 BRL B28295 and Mary Wright, *Montpelier, Decades of Protest* p 115. p71; Wright points out that the campaigning pressure group had to concentrate its efforts on increasing support among Labour councillors – as being the party most likely to change its official policy

14. *Ibid*

15. Mary Wright, *Montpelier, Decades of Protest* p 116

16. More about the Festival in Chapter 8

17. Methodist Church Centenary leaflet

18. eg. 1974 when next year's budget was being prepared, tensions showed in the comment 'Much of the information which has now been gathered should have been available from previous from previous authorities at least a year ago'. There were two trivial examples in Totterdown – one was in 1969 over which council was responsible for cutting the newly planted grass on the core site prairie; the other was over the removal of the former road widening line on St Luke's Road noted in Chapter 3, 'Changes in Local Government'. Possibly they bonded over the job of redevelopment in Totterdown when a wide cross section of committees had to work together to make it happen

19. The LUTS Report was still awaited - the first draft was published in 1975

20. David Starkie, *The Motorway Age* pp 78, 79 Pergamon Press 1982

21. BRL BL 17D: *The Fight for Bristol* pp 98

22. This is a question Tony Benn won't answer directly but he sent copies of his *Guardian* articles on transport in 1963 and '64 to speak for themselves, with a note reading: 'Undoubtedly Government policy was influenced by pressure and that is always the case'

23. Mary Wright: *Montpelier* p117. Re: expense: apart from the land acquisition, the flats were estimated by the Council's critics to cost £9k per bedroom

24. See Chapter 3, 'Blight in Totterdown'

25. In the second half of the 1970s, the legacy of city wide destruction and neglect was addressed by the creation of more conservation areas and some government grants available for their upkeep. *The Fight for Bristol* p115

26. This is to underestimate changes in politics, the protest movement and the growth of democracy by the 70s; but the availability of boom finance had been central to the great 60s Planning Disasters and bust budgets were central to their cancellation or modification

27. *Bush Telegraph* 1980

28. BEP 11 January 1980 BRL B32466

29. BEP 13 May 1980 BRL B32466

30. ACC Planning and Highways Committee 672 March 1980

31. BEP 9 October 1980 BRL B32466

Chapter 6

1. See Chapter 5, 17: Methodist Church Centenary leaflet

2. BRL AN 27127001, 'How it Happened in Totterdown', George Micklewright, 1981

3. Believing it was the path to prosperity and prestige. Mary Wright, *Montpelier*, p 114

4. BRL B27809, City and Council of Bristol proposed Outer Circuit Road Stages 2 & 3, Freeman Fox and Partners

5. ACC 672 P&H Committee February 1980

6. BRL B27809 Freeman Fox etc plans

7. The Council would also buy homes of people who wanted to move out of the area completely.

8. Redland Housing Association had recently been set up in the mid 1970s and this was its first big job. It acquired many new houses in Totterdown whilst working on the Action Area, see 7

9. *Bush Telegraph* May 1978, p 7

10. *Ibid*

11. *The Finger Post* July 1988 p 7. *Finger Post* was a local newsletter produced for several years by Kim and Norm Brooks and the Music project

12. The *Finger Post*, August 1988 p 13

13. BEP 22 May 1985 BRL B32466

14. *Western Daily Press,* 14 August 1981 BRL B32466

Chapter 7

1. 558, Land & Buildings Committee 1983/4 Vol I, September 1984

2. Pam Tatlow, Councillor, Windmill Hill. *Finger Post* Nov 88 pp1-2

Chapter 8

1. Playworker: Paul Dielhem *The Finger Post* July 1988 p.1 Google Totterdown Children's Workshop for the last Auction and see what had been donated to auction!

2. All of this section is taken from TACA's archive, dates, see TACA website

3. *Bush Telegraph* November 1975

4. Our Forgotten Heritage, Max Barnes, reproduced in Knowledge no 1-6 Knowle Library

5. ISBN 0-85054-892-6 Old Ordnance Survey Maps, Bristol SE on the reverse

Chapter 9

1. Google Goole Action Group then to Office of the Deputy Prime Minister: Housing for latest news

2. Google Welsh Streets Home Group then follow link to Office of the Deputy Prime Minister: Housing

3. Google Welsh Streets Liverpool and follow any number of links for latest news

4. PR/004350; BOV/NVP/ 000006; DBN/000280;DBN/000516